THE INTERIM
IS MINE

First edition: Budgate Press 2010
All rights reserved
budgate@gmail.com

Budgate Press
Postnet Suite 402
Constantia 7848
Cape Town
Republic of South Africa

Subject: Political Science: History & Theory - General

ISBN: 978-0-620-48618-7
Printed by Lightning Source

THE INTERIM
IS MINE

IAN DALLAS

Robert Devereaux, 2nd Earl of Essex.

"When nobility is suppressed –
All government is subverted."

Robert Devereux,
Earl of Essex.

CONTENTS

I

THE PATTERN
OF POWER

Today people discourse on the subject of how to recover and continue the very social ethos that is in the penultimate phase of the destruction of both the planet and the human species.

The message of the nihilists is that you will not succeed in rescue by the destruction of the social ethos since the essential programme of that social ethos is, itself, destruction. It follows that nihilism is the core doctrine of the present society which only invites the participant to complete the annihilation consciously and not, as at present, unconsciously.

The foundational document of nihilism is Dostoevsky's 'Crime and Punishment'. Its policies and practices received their primal expression in the novels of Turgenev, and within the ethos of nihilism itself came the great analysis of it in action both in the 'Ring' of Wagner and in the monumental prose plays of Ibsen.

The pivotal dynamic of the nihil in Dostoevsky's novel is not that the man commits a murder but rather that given the act of murder it is voided of meaning and detached from the rational linear pattern of prior conditions, a culminant action, and a resultant situation. In Gide's appreciation of the book he particularised this action without meaning or sequential effect as an 'acte gratuite'. While nihilism manifested in a political design its core was a fractured individual psyche. 'The Possessed' was the social sickness but Raskolnikov was the patient himself.

It follows from this that a social fabric is dependent on the societal individual and his programme stems from himself. Yet he is a product as well as producer of the social nexus. In other words we cannot trace the social malaise to a psychological manifestation. What we now know is that the web of civic practice affects the genetic design of the individual. It is this profound awareness which illuminates Ibsen's 'Ghosts' and

makes it a pivotal document of our epoch, mis-
understood as it was when it emerged, seen only as
a morality play.

Sir Julian Huxley, the grandson of T. H. Huxley
and the brother of Aldous Huxley whose study of
a eugenic state, 'Brave New World', still stands
unconfronted, in a lecture to the British Eugenics
Society took up the Darwinian discourse. He
argued that genetic deterioration was taking place
in modern populations as a result of the relaxation
of natural selection and of the inverse relationship
between social class and fertility. He stated that:

> "Deleterious mutations far outnumber
> useful ones. There is an inherent tendency
> for the hereditary constitution to degrade
> itself. In wild animals and plants this
> tendency is either reversed or at least held
> in check by the operation of natural select-
> ion and, in domestic animals and plants, the
> same result is achieved by our artificial
> selection. But in civilised human communi-
> ties of our present type, the elimination of
> defect by natural selection is largely (though
> of course by no means wholly) rendered
> inoperative by medicine, charity, and the

social services, while, as we have seen, there is no selection encouraging favourable variations. The net result is that many deleterious mutations can and do survive, and the tendency to degradation of the gene-plasm can manifest itself. Today, thanks to the last 15 years' work in pure science, we can be sure of this alarming fact, whereas previously it was only a vague surprise. Humanity will gradually destroy itself from within, will decay in its very core and essence, if this slow but insidious relentless process is not checked. Here again, dealing with defectives in the present system can be at best a palliative. We must be able to pick out the genetically inferior stocks with more certainty, and we must set in motion counter-forces making for faster reproduction of superior stocks, if we are to reverse or even arrest the trend."

Darwin by 1871 had seen the dilemma. In 'The Descent of Man' he had written:

"We civilised men do our utmost to check the process of elimination: we build asylums for the imbecile, the maimed and the sick: we institute poor laws, and our medical men exert their utmost skills to save the life of everyone to the last moment. Thus the weak members of civilised societies propagate their kind. No-one will doubt that this must be highly injurious to the race of man."

A breakdown in natural selection means that mankind has ceased to evolve. Ironically, medical progress continues to mean genetic deterioration.

The eugenicists' claim is that the modern populations are deteriorating genetically, and this, on the basis of the research evidence.

The eugenicists believe that thinking people should consider what policies might be formulated to correct this so that, as Galton originally put it, the failure of natural selection could be compensated by consciously designed selection.

The eugenicists have also claimed that the world would be a better place if people were free of genetic diseases, mental retardation, stupidity, anti-social behaviour and crime.

As the great structuration leadership of a new society after World War Two set about its plans for a world whose mass would be static and obedient, while its oligarchy would be mobile and independent, in the formulation of an acquisitive programme that would mathematically scoop the world's wealth into its hands by a simply binary information system whose institutions were corporate structures and whose instruments of wealth would be numeric contracts, themselves worthless but protected by their inner dynamic of increase in every transaction favouring the financial system, that same structuration could not tolerate any introduction of value measurement, character confirmation or genuine elitist transcendence of its own oligarchic hegemony.

History, social patterning, individual quality, brotherhood, real-value wealth, and the very genetic foundation of the individual and the group were declared out of order in the discourse.

It was simply enough to denounce any social doctrine as fascist to have it swept aside. Unfortunately this meant that the new monetarists had a means of imposing a unitary world view which uncritically confirmed corporation capitalism as it could freely fling out any challenge to it as, by definition, fascist. Later, the silenced 'other' of bankism was communist. This lasted until the fall of its Russian regime. Then, bankism faced up to a much more dangerous 'other', one which claimed a Divine and Prophetic authority. Islam.

By the opening of the 21st Century it was becoming clear that the internal logic of an investment wealth system implied from its beginning that the bank would become a global 24 hour market which would inevitably move from project to super-project, from bank to super-bank, and therefore from basket-currencies to one world currency and finally to a wholly owned market entity which in turn could simply abolish money itself.

It was inside this spiralling plunge into world-population debt to the oligarchic banks that, finally, people began to realise that the world-system was not for people – only an oligarchic, increasingly reduced oligarchic dictatorship. The materialist and godless new society had turned the human population at large into slaves – only now they were called debtors. Every child now born into the world emerges not as a free creature in a free world but as a debtor owing an unpayable sum to finance through belonging to a nation or state, itself already indebted or bankrupt.

History had to be abolished as an instrument of study since it indicated that things were not always thus. In other words, the present state of perpetual financial crisis was not the state of nature itself, but rather the disastrous achievement of men.

Equally, anthropology had to be abolished as an instrument of study since it indicated that men had not originally been blocked in mass-groupings of states, interlocked by fiduciary contracts whose protocols were kept secret from them. Men had once lived in organic patterns of tribes and clans, cities and terrains. The order of their lives only half-understood but rhythmically adhered to in all matters of genetic bonding, inheritance, frontiers and possessions.

Man had become a genetic Robinson Crusoe cut off from his past, his family, its story and its identity.

The lie of modernity is that men lived in primitive social structures bonded by tribal allegiances and enmity, moving across the earth in search of new resources while today men live in structurally designed states, called nations, decision-making in the hands of an elite chosen by the mass of the populace, the pragmatism of survival having been displaced by the mathematical structuring of social processes.

At the very moment that the genetic code of the

species has been discovered, the same species under the imperatives of its economic doctrines has abolished the social patterning of births, marriages and inheritance.

A group of anthropologists spent long months in the Amazon forests trying to break the complex coding of one jungle community, which, given its small population had evaded the expected price of inter-breeding – mongolism, albinism and idiocy. The marriage and inheritance laws seemed indecipherable. Having failed in their research they took off for civilisation in a plane which, departing, flew over the village of their studies. As the scientists looked down on the mud huts, laid out in geometric order, one of the researchers called out: "Of course! The village IS the genetic code." The layout of the houses indicated which man could be married to which woman, what cross-overs were permitted and which forbidden.

This, in Islamic thinking, is called 'FITRA' or primal nature, or that culture pattern of early men which functioned because in harmony with nature or rather the natural process.

When the woman leader of the British government declared a war on a distant land to assure her re-election this was a woman appointed to high office by the random system of mass universal franchise (Bernard Shaw's "Anybody chosen by everybody"). Years later her son was arrested and convicted as an international terrorist plotting a coup d'état in an African state.

The mother had been raised up by a valueless system of number superiority. The son was a genetic determinacy, of low-life stock in high probability heading for crime. He was the proof of the false system of leadership choice which had resulted in an unworthy leader. In Wordsworth's phrase: "The child is father of the man," or woman in this case.

Genealogy is therefore a science of probability. The low genetic line of the criminal son was that of a low intelligence mother and an alcoholic father. What emerges is that the genetic inheritance is affected, altered, improved or degraded by the civic mores under which the new human entity is reared. The racehorse is the result of both careful breeding and expert training. The recovery of the human species from its present devolution requires controlled union and guided upbringing. In the case of the humans personal education is, by definition, also social. Not just an educational group but a social nexus is required to fashion humans of quality.

The marital bond is foundational to social harmony and survival. This must not be taken in a bourgeois or Victorian sense. This recognition of marriage is based on a society taking on and respecting its pattern. The monogamism of the christians has degenerated into the individualist contractless 'relationship', itself a commercial term.

The biological drive of the male human is to diversity in order to allow his maximum reproductive expression. The biological drive of the female human is to security and protection of her offspring, this is seen as faithfulness. Any social order that takes into cognizance these fundamental human characteristics will flourish. Monogamy imposed by celibate and thus misogynistic priests led to a sub-culture of mistresses and an under-culture of prostitution. The balanced and median culture decreed by Islam lies half-way between the repressive and un-natural monogamy of christianity and the polygamous pattern of primitive cultures. The four wife household of a fully functioning Muslim society is both social and private.

Once the legal norm of marriage is imposed on a society the obligations and implications define the societal patterns of possession and exchange.

It is because marriage as an institution, for it is

essentially a financial institution, has been abolished that modern men, while they may fight as slave mercenaries, cannot fight wars. Corporations make wars. Men have been rendered passive as consumers and miners. In other words, un-manned, lacking a societal group identity. This is the atheist global situation. Only a Divine-worshipping society can recover the categorical imperatives of the human species in evolution again.

As marriage is recovered it will be seen again not as a fantasy of romantic love in the modern manufactured mode of the cinema's individualist values, but as a contract, and that not even a civic but a fiduciary contract. Marriage joins two capital units of both wealth and property. The tragedy of 'Romeo and Juliet' is not their suicide, itself abhorrent and foolish, but rather that their folly – romantic love – prevents the union of the Montagues and the Capulets.

The marriage contract in itself defines expansion, whether of property, land or goods. In the current usury-banking society increase is achieved by divorce, the pre-nuptial agreement assuring in advance the benefits of divorce. While the stability of marriage exists as a structural element of society the meaning and evaluation of life can be experienced at a personal and existential level. Once divorce emerges as the norm, or marriage is replaced by the 'relationship', itself a fleeting and undefined condition, the result is the isolated individual, and as such, the isolated individual is helpless to create a societal model. Marriage and inheritance – joining and transfer – are thus the warp and woof of the community.

The contractual basis of marriage in turn determines the continuity of the societal template. It not only confers legitimacy on the heirs, it excludes access to the results of the flaunting and devaluing of the original marriage contract and thus marriage as a working model. Bastardy did not de-value the bastard but it did dislocate him from the societal order of expansion. Marriage not only grants order to the future, that is the on-going continuity of the family, it also verifies its historicity.

Important families, that is inheritors of name, place and influence, have in the past always recorded the history of their former generations. Since bastardy and usurpation are the natural corollary of marriage and inheritance, the record of contract and transfer has always been maintained for the security of the social nexus.

In England, the crises of state occurred around

legitimacy of rule and inheritance. The Plantagenet dynasty collapsed over these issues. The country had been ruled by tribal Saxon warlords and Danish invaders until the Norman Conquest. This feudalised England and brought a sophisticated legal system, language and a new aristocracy. The Treaty of Wallingford confirmed Henry of Anjou, a Norman Duke, as King of England. Taking the family emblematic plant as the dynasty's name, the Plantagenets came to rule England. They were to rule for over 300 years. For over 200 of these years the crown passed, in a general peace, from father to son. One of the greatest dynasties in world history, it in due course broke on the key issue of governance, legitimacy. The great family split into two houses, Lancaster and York, and they clashed in civil war, known as the Wars of the Roses. The Plantagenet dynasty ended with the death of Richard III. The power passed to the Tudors under Henry VII.

The Tudors were from bastard stock. Henry VII's mother, Margaret Beaufort, was a descendant of John Beaufort, the natural son of John of Gaunt, Duke of Lancaster and his mistress, Katherine Swynford. Henry's father, Edmund Tudor, was the offspring of the liaison between Henry V's widow,

Katherine of France, and the Welsh squire, Owen Tudor. Their children were considered to be bastards therefore denied inheritance. Despite his ineligibility to claim the throne, Henry Tudor remained the natural heir to the Lancastrian claim to kingship. To strengthen his position he married Elizabeth of York, daughter of Edward IV, thus uniting the red and white roses of Lancaster and York. Henry's crown was validated by right of conquest – he dated his reign from the day before the Battle of Bosworth where he defeated Richard III and not from his marriage to Elizabeth of York. Right of conquest is the ownership of land passing to the victor, thus, inheritance. Marriage and inheritance – joining and transfer – as we have indicated are the twin dynamics of society.

The Tudor dynasty can now be seen as the triumphant high point of English society. The dynasty lasted 118 years. Yet on Henry VII's accession to the throne there were 18 people with a greater right to it than he. Henry adopted two political strategies to confer legitimacy on his reign. He traced in his Welsh forebears a direct line to King Arthur, the ancient British ruler, and the Welsh Prince Cadwaladr. He set the Welsh dragon on his standard and added to this a cult of chivalry and its medieval sports which at the same time tuned a new loyal aristocracy to the Tudor throne.

As a result of this chivalric ethos, which brought honour, nobility and loyalty to the nation's elite, he established an iconography of family identity and connection. Heraldry became an instrument of political power.

In Jessie Childs' study of the foolish Earl of Surrey, son of the Duke of Norfolk, she writes:

"Surrey was accused of the lèse-majesté of bearing the arms of Edward the Confessor. This is not as extraordinary as it may sound. In sixteenth-century England, where the majority of the population was illiterate, the power of image was tremendous. The Flodden Duke's funeral, Holbein's portrait of Henry VIII at Whitehall, the Tournament of May 1540 and the ceremonies and insignia of the Order of the Garter are just a few of the instances of the potency of symbolism and spectacle in this age. Coats of arms were not just adornments, but vivid expressions of lineage, identity and power. The image of Edward the Confessor symbolised sanctity, legitimacy and majesty. Most English Kings were crowned (using his regalia) and buried at Westminster Abbey, where his shrine lay. Five English Kings had been named after him and

Henry VIII maintained the tradition with his heir." Childs defines Surrey's crime as "heraldic violation".

The death of Richard III does not lead on smoothly to the opening of the Tudor Dynasty. The great Plantagenet reign itself was split in two. The murder of Richard II saw the end of their direct line. Richard was deposed and probably murdered by his cousin, Bolingbroke. Thus the last of the dynasty is only in the cousinage, leaving Henry IV the usurper insecure in his inheritance. From Henry VI to Richard III was a disintegration that ended in the civil war of the two Houses claiming sovereignty. It is this chronicle of dynasty, legitimacy, usurpation and conquest that gave to Shakespeare his epic cycle of History Plays.

However, the unfolding of the applied laws of legitimacy, inheritance and conquest is not merely a monolinear system of genealogical hegemony – essential to it, not just a civic background but as living dynamic, is the rise, growth and demise of a way of life and evaluation called chivalry.

Chivalry began and evolved as a uniquely secular organisational procedure which after its triumphant flowering was to see its demise caused by the Church's infiltration and eventual deconstruction of it. It is important, as we shall see, to grasp that its sources and evaluations were not christian and indeed rendered the Church irrelevant. Chivalry was involved in the formation of an elite brotherhood under arms, bonded together by the mutually upheld set of high moral behavioural values.

Its exclusivity and honour was delineated outwardly by the complex semiotic science of heraldry which indicated primarily the bloodline of the participant and secondarily the military allegiance of the knight.

Inwardly it was preserved by the membership of a chivalric Order, adherence to which entailed the undertaking of the high moral practices demanded of the brothers. The most famous of these were the Order of the Garter, Order of the Star and Order of the Golden Fleece, but as these Orders became public domain involving Church and State we can discern a quite discrete system uniting a hidden Order of a very different kind that set itself at odds with the Roman Church and its belief system.

The vowed obligations of the chivalric knight were the same in every situation. They were:

> Prouesse
> Loyauté

> Largesse
> Courtoisie
> Franchise

Ghillebert de Lannoy, for example, ordered his son to take up:

> Martial training
> Jousting
> The company of the Bons
>   Saiges
>   Courtois
>   Preux
>   Vaillans

Wolfram von Eschenbach recorded that: "Wille-ham addressed his Knights, saying: 'There are two rewards that await us – heaven and the recognition of noble women.'"

The great treatise on chivalry which became almost standardised across Europe was written between 1165 and 1185 by Chrétien de Troyes. It is important to understand that the political emergence of the rites and practices of chivalry took place against the background of a Europe oriented towards an ongoing programme of Crusades. The

Crusader ethos could be likened to the Cold War mentality which ran through both the thinking, the practice and the imagining of several generations during the 20th century.

It would be very naive to think that the militant conflict between the Papal Church and the Muslim community implied a mutual ignorance between the two parties. Both sides saw prisoners, taken, ransomed and sometimes absorbed. By the end of the chivalric age the great writers of Europe were utterly conversant with Islam, its beliefs and its people. From Dante to Shakespeare and Marlowe there is on record a remarkable grasp of the enemy religion. Over these centuries is a trail of intellectual exchange, marriage, trade and diplomatic agreements.

One such exchange can be seen as revealing two things. Firstly, the martial codes of the two antagonists were both similar and quite different. Thus, there was discourse between them. Secondly, it showed that while there was amity between the two warrior elites, the Papal Church was opposed to this harmony and ruthlessly re-wrote and re-designed anything that might point towards an adoption of the Islamic model.

In one of the battles of the Crusaders with the

great Muslim monarch, Salahud-din, or as the christians called him, Saladin, a knight taken prisoner was put up for ransom. During his detention he met and dined with his Muslim captor.

They talked. In their talk Saladin initiated his prisoner into the ethos of their chivalry. Such was the harmony between them that after Saladin had taken him into his confidence he released him in order that he could transmit to his fellow knights the chivalric roots of Islamic war and peace. Saladin paid to his wazir the knight's ransom money. Of course, the horrified Roman hierarchy took his evidence and re-wrote it as a christian tract, implying that the christian Crusader was educating the Muslim warlord.

This was against a background of how things already were, it was neither anomalous nor strange, but rather part of the state of things.

Queen Joan, the sister of the Crusader King Richard I, was married to William of Sicily. She had two servants that were Muslim. On her husband's death her brother as he passed through Sicily took her with him and escorted her to the Crusading army. Her two servants crossed over, were given a most kindly welcome, and when they came to join the Muslim army Sultan Saladin loaded them with marks of his favour.

Sultan Saladin was in correspondence with the ruler in Constantinople and negotiated to have the Khutba pronounced from the mosque there in the name of the Abbasid Khalif. In other words, despite the relentless censorship and distortions of the Roman Church and its inquisitional policies there was a constant flow of communication between the Muslims and Europe.

Let us, therefore, examine the content of what the learned warrior, liberator of Jerusalem, conveyed to his captive christian knight.

II

WHAT SALADIN SAID

Allah, the Exalted, says in the Qur'an (20:134):

> "Say: 'Everyone is waiting expectantly
> so wait expectantly.
> You will soon know
> who are the Companions of the Right Path
> and who is guided.'"

The Messenger of Allah, may Allah bless him and grant him peace, said:

> "The Deen is behaviour."

The Deen is not merely religion and its rites. It has a deeper meaning – and that is 'the life-transaction'.

Allah, the Exalted, says in the Qur'an (2:245):

> Their Prophet said to them,
> 'Allah has appointed Talut to be your king.'
> They said, 'How can he have kingship over us
> when we have much more right to kingship
>   than he does?
> He has not even got much wealth!'
> He said, 'Allah has chosen him over you
> and favoured him greatly in knowledge
>   and physical strength.
> Allah gives kingship to anyone He wills.
> Allah is All-Encompassing, All-Knowing.'

Abu'd-Darda' said: "The Prophets are the pegs which hold the earth in place. When Prophethood was brought to an end, Allah replaced the Prophets with some of the people from the Community of Muhammad, may Allah bless him and grant him peace, called Abdal.

They are not superior to other people in respect of fasting or prayer, but on account of their good character, true scrupulousness, good intention, sound hearts and good counsel for all the Muslims, seeking Allah's pleasure by steadfastness, forbearance, intelligence and humility without abasement.

They are the khalifs of the Prophets, the people Allah has chosen for Himself and whom He has selected for Himself by His knowledge. They are forty true men. Thirty of them have a similar certainty to that of Ibrahim, the Friend of the All-Merciful. By them Allah drives away disliked things from the people of the earth and innovations which people have introduced. It is because of them that people have rain and provision. None of them dies without Allah putting someone else in his place."

Sufyan ath-Thawri said: "They are the means by which the Deen is established."

Let us return to the matter of kingship in the story of Talut.

Allah, the Exalted, declares in the Qur'an (2:246):

> Their Prophet said to them,
> 'The sign of his kingship is
>   that the Ark will come to you,
> containing serenity from your Lord
> and certain relics left

    by the families of Musa and Harun.
It will be borne by angels.
There is a sign for you in that
    if you are muminun.'

The serenity – Sakina – Ibn Abbas said that it was
a gold basin from the Garden in which the hearts
of the Prophets were washed.

The Qur'an continues (2:247):

When Talut marched out with the army,
    he said,
'Allah will test you with a river.
Anyone who drinks from it is not with me.
But anyone who does not taste it is with me –
except for him who merely scoops up a little
    in his hand.'
But they drank from it –
    except for a few of them.
Then when he and those who had iman
    with him had crossed it,
they said, 'We do not have the strength
to face Goliath and his troops today.'
But those who were sure
    that they were going to meet Allah

said, 'How many a small force
   has triumphed over
a much greater one by Allah's permission!
Allah is with the steadfast.'

Now we know that the small force which will
triumph over the ignorant masses is able to succeed
because, banded together, obedient to their leader,
they have set themselves the highest standard. Let
us examine the core of the matter.

Allah, the Exalted, says in the Qur'an (18:9):

Do you consider that the Companions of the
Cave and Ar-Raqim
were one of the most remarkable
   of Our Signs?

The Raqim was the tablet on which their names
and lineages were written.

Here we come upon the source of the spring of all
chivalry. Allah, the Exalted, says in the Qur'an
(18:10):

When the noble young men took refuge in

the cave and said,
'Our Lord, give us mercy directly from You
and open the way for us to right guidance
    in our situation.'

The word used here is 'fitya', the plural of 'fata',
meaning a perfect young man. The important thing
to grasp is that to have such a 'fata' it is necessary
to have him in the plural – 'fitya' is therefore the
special group of excellence which is needed that
mankind may be in turn ennobled.

The narrative continues in the Qur'an (18:11-26):

So We sealed their ears with sleep
in the cave for a number of years.
Then We woke them up again
so that we might see which of the two groups
would better calculate
    the time they had stayed there.

We will relate their story to you with truth.
They were young men
    who had iman in their Lord
and We increased them in guidance.
We fortified their hearts

when they stood up and said,
'Our Lord is the Lord of the heavens
  and the earth
and We will not call on any god
  apart from Him.
We would in that case have uttered
  an abomination.
These people of ours have taken gods
  apart from Him.
Why do they not produce
  a clear authority concerning them?
Who could do greater wrong than someone
who invents a lie against Allah?
When you have separated yourselves from
them and everything they worship except
Allah, take refuge in the cave
and your Lord will unfold His mercy to you
and open the way to the best for you
  in your situation.'

You would have seen the sun, when it rose,
inclining away from their cave towards the
right, and, when it set, leaving them behind
on the left, while they were lying in
  an open part of it.
That was one of Allah's Signs.

Whoever Allah guides is truly guided.
But if He misguides someone,
you will find no protector for them
to guide them rightly.
You would have supposed them to be awake
whereas in fact they were asleep.
We moved them to the right and to the left,
and, at the entrance, their dog
   stretched out its paws.
If you had looked down and seen them,
you would have turned from them and run
and have been filled with terror
   at the sight of them.

That was the situation when we woke them up
so they could question one another.
One of them asked,
'How long have you been here?'
They replied,
'We have been here for a day or part of a day.'
They said, 'Your Lord knows best how long
you have been here.
Send one of your number into the city
with this silver you have,
so he can see which food is purest
   and bring you some of it to eat.

But he should go about with caution
so that no one is aware of you,
for if they find out about you they will stone
you or make you revert to their religion
and then you will never have success.'
Accordingly We made them chance upon
them unexpectedly
so they might know
that Allah's promise is true
and that there is no doubt about the Hour.
When they were arguing among themselves
about the matter, they said,
'Wall up their cave,
their Lord knows best about them.'
But those who got the better of the argument
concerning them said,
'We will build a place of worship over them.'

They will say, 'There were three of them,
their dog being the fourth.'
They will say, 'There were five of them,
their dog being the sixth,'
guessing at the Unseen.
And they will say, 'There were seven of them,
their dog being the eighth.'
Say: 'My Lord knows best their number.

Those who know about them are very few.'
So do not enter into any argument
   concerning them,
except in relation to what is clearly known.
And do not seek the opinion of any of them
regarding them.

Never say about anything,
'I am doing that tomorrow,'
without adding 'If Allah wills.'
Remember your Lord when you forget,
and say, 'Hopefully my Lord will guide me
to something closer
   to right guidance than this.'

They stayed in their Cave
for three hundred years
and added nine.
Say: 'Allah knows best how long they stayed.
The Unseen of the heavens and the earth
belongs to Him.
How perfectly He sees, how well He hears!
They have no protector apart from Him.
Nor does He share His rule with anyone.'

Now that you have recognised the existence of a

brotherhood in every age to be witness to the truth you have to face up to the reality of the presence of the lord 'Isa, Jesus, on earth as both a mortal man and a Messenger of Allah.

Once the truth of Jesus is known the subsequent doctrine of the so-called Sacrament simply collapses. And then, only then, does the great miracle appear which lays open a future world of chivalric nobility, respect for women, and guardianship of the poor.

Here is the news.

Allah, the Exalted, declares in the Qur'an (4:155-7):

> And on account of their kufr,
> and their utterance
> of a monstrous slander against Maryam,
> and their saying, 'We killed the Messiah,
> 'Isa son of Maryam, Messenger of Allah.'
> They did not kill him
> and they did not crucify him
> but it was made to seem so to them.
> Those who argue about him
>   are in doubt about it.
> They have no real knowledge of it,

just conjecture.
But they certainly did not kill him.
Allah raised him up to Himself.
Allah is Almighty, All-Wise.

It follows from this that the fundamental lie of the Papal Catholic Church is that the following deception was played out.

Firstly, the mortal Messenger is renamed as 'the Son' of God. Then he is crucified, shedding his blood to 'save' mankind. His very flesh is a sacrifice.

Secondly, this is ritualised in a gathering of disciples where Jesus is supposed to have declared the bread as his body and the wine as his blood. With the Latin 'hic est corpus', the magical sacramental rite is established on a dual premiss: that the bread and wine are, not as symbol, or as memorial but as fact transformed into the flesh and blood of Jesus.

The second part being that those who partake of this anthropophagy are saved from damnation in the Next World. In turn, this demands that only an initiate priesthood can enact the transformative act and thus the Christian Church is formed, not in Jerusalem, but Rome. And so, by a magical wave of the arm in a cross-like gesture, the Rome of the

Caesars becomes the Rome of the Popes.

If that were the whole of the matter then it would appear that the world had been plunged into a dark deception that could only end in total nihilism.

Against this lie, the Qur'an also revealed what in fact had happened, and how that in turn was transmuted back into a distorted version of the pure miracle, and that lie was the Mesa of blood sacrifice.

The true event is luminous and beautiful, as truth is.

Allah, the Exalted, says in the Qur'an (5:112-115):

> And when the Disciples said,
> "Isa son of Maryam!
> Can your Lord send down a table to us
>   out of heaven?'
> He said,
> 'Have taqwa of Allah if you are muminun!'
>
> They said, 'We want to eat from it
> and for our hearts to be at peace
> and to know that you have told us the truth
> and to be among those who witness it.'

'Isa son of Maryam said, 'Allah, our Lord,
send down a table to us out of heaven
to be a feast for us,
for the first and last of us,
and as a Sign from You.
Provide for us!
You are the Best of Providers!'
Allah said, 'I will send it down to you
but if anyone among you is kafir after that,
I will punish him with a punishment
   the like of which
I will not inflict on anyone else
   in all the worlds!'

The term 'kafir' refers to those who cover up the truth and deny what is true. The invention that the table was to host magical bread and wine that throughout centuries would turn into the cellular blood and tissue of Jesus was the cover-up of all subsequent history.

In these three passages of the final revealed Book there remain embodied the means – by the Qur'anic truth – to set up an elite community which can stand against the monstrous evil of Popes, initiating Bishops, and corrupt Priests, and the quotidian evidence against them will be their misogyny and their unnatural celibacy.

So, let the noblest of the knights and the bravest of the most ancient families hold together in loyalty, and goodness, and courtesy to protect the true values of the eternal truth, and ancient wisdom, for while it goes back to the first peoples it must survive for the time when the Last Message reaches all the world amid the ruins of the two atheisms, christianity and the worship of the masses.

Let us forge guarded circles – a fraternity of truth.

III

THE CHIVALRIC ORDER
AS ANTI-ROME

So it was that with all the inevitable meetings between Muslims and christians caused by the bloody and futile adventures of Crusading, slowly, battle by battle, encounter by encounter the European structuralist super-state of Papal christendom was infiltrated and taught the lessons of Islamic brotherhood and leadership. The result was that by the time of the Tudor Dynasty there was a deep and utterly aware intellectual grasp of Islam both as Deen and as social nexus, as can be witnessed in the delightfully ambiguous loyalty to both religions in the plays of Christopher Marlowe.

Over these five hundred years from Saladin to the Tudors, the aristocratic leadership of Europe had forged a completely independent and opposite religion to the cross and blood sacrifice doctrines of Papal Rome. Over these centuries the Church persisted in penetrating this other religion both by torture and execution and by attempting to smother its heraldic outward display in crosses, crucifixes and Saint-days.

They tried to eliminate the chivalric tournament again and again as they tried to ban the bullfight with its calls of "Allah!" and its turbaned toreros, finally submitting to what had been a chivalric test of battle by holding it on Saint-days and making the sign of the cross its good-luck charm.

Pope Innocent II had the tournament condemned in the ninth canon of the Council of Clermont in 1130 and commanded that knights who were killed in tournaments should not be given Christian burial. The ban was re-enshrined in Papal law by each succeeding Pope, each one more ferocious all the way to Clement V. In the end John XXII finally had to give up and lift the ban in 1316. The last attempt to stifle the practice of tournaments lay in the decision to adapt it to serve the Papal system. It would be used to inspire men to set out on the

Crusades, itself a counter-productive solution for two reasons. One, it led to tournaments being performed by the knights of local Syrian and Palestinian princes. Two, it continued that cross-fertilisation between Islam and christianity that was the inevitable by-product of these wars.

Put at its essential issue – knights dedicated to honour, valour and victory loathed with all their militant being a religion based on a man nailed to a cross. It was repellent because of its utter helplessness. It was a symbol of defeat and disgrace.

The chivalric Order was based on a limited number of noble youths – the Companions of the Cave – their number still argued over. They re-appeared again and again as 'the Neuf Preux' in poems extolling their nobility. They appear on tapestries and wall-paintings, they become the heroes of chivalric adventures. In France the Constable du Guesclin was named as the Tenth 'Preux'. In Scotland, Robert the Bruce was hailed as one of the 'Companions'.

The circle of loyalty and prowess was represented by the King and the knights of his Round Table, the Table from heaven at which a blessed meal was taken. In its centre was the Golden Dish from which the Knights feasted, a feast on which descended the heavenly peace, the Sakina.

The Roman Church had a consistory of scholars employed in re-designing the dangerous myth and reality of the Knights of the Round Table and the Golden Dish from which emanated Divine serenity. It gradually was christianised with the Blood Sacrament being centred on the holy platter now transformed into a chalice, containing the blood of Jesus. Thus came the invention of the Holy Grail.

Of course, even this christian version traces back to the Knights Templar whose Order was disbanded and its leadership accused of having crossed over to the religion of Islam. They were nearly all burned at the stake as Muslims. The Grail Castle of Munsalvesche in Wolfram's 'Parzifal' is guarded by Templars on the frontier between christian and Muslim Spain.

The Teutonic Knights, the famous German military Order, had taken as its model the Knights Templar. Under their Grand Master Winrich von Kniprode who ruled from 1351 to 1382 the Order recruited Knights from across Europe to conquer the pagan eastern lands. The terrain of Eastern Europe was wild and difficult to traverse. They called it the Wilderness and an expedition was called a Reise. To bind the Knights in harmony of purpose a Table of Honour would be prepared for the most prestigious of the Knights.

The 'Ehrentisch', the Table of Honour, was described at the Council of Constance by a Polish witness:

> "The brothers of the Order prepared a solemn feast for a certain number of such persons or guests, say for ten or twelve or some other small number. Only those persons who were selected from among the Knights by the heralds there present were assigned to places at the Table."

In the Chronique du Bon Duc Loys de Bourbon it tells how the Grand Master spread the Ehrentisch for Knights from several kingdoms.

> "Two each up to twelve, and thanks be to God to those twelve they explained this Order of the Table and how it came to be established. And then one of the Knights of that region gave to each of them a shoulder badge on which was written in letters of gold, 'Honneur vainc tout!'"

Across Europe existed an elite religion based on the honour, nobility and military courage of its members, people of the Table, the Ehrentisch, as was the Knight in the Prologue of Chaucer's 'Canterbury Tales', the "very parfit gentil Knight."

The final element of the new chivalric religion, having replaced a celibate and misogynist priesthood with a new elite brotherhood of warriors, was to introduce the honour due to women. Women were pure by nature and not, as the priests claimed, corrupted vessels of the flesh pulling men down to punishment and death. Part of chivalry was not only the respect due to good women but also the task of protecting them from slander and danger.

This last chivalric doctrine of the Knights was to be met with the unrelenting persecution, torture and burning of women, at its height naming them as witches of the Devil.

In all of this we can discern a dynamic form, not just of a brotherhood elite but of a key qualitative bonding which is at the same time the core of the Divine transaction set up among peoples and also the core evaluation of which civilisation itself is the by-product.

From the ancient narration of the Companions of the Cave to the twelve Disciples of the Messenger

of God, Jesus ('Isa), on to the ten Companions of
the Final Messenger of Allah.

In At-Tirmidhi it is recorded:

> Salih bin Mismar al-Maruzi related to us
> from Ibn Abi Fudayn, from Musa bin
> Ya'qub, from Umar bin Sa'id, from Abdar-
> rahman bin Humayd, from his father, from
> Sa'd bin Zayd, about a group of the Com-
> panions of the Messenger of Allah. The
> Messenger said, "Ten are in the Garden.
> Abu Bakr is in the Garden, Umar is in the
> Garden. And Uthman, 'Ali, Az-Zubayr,
> Talha, Abdarrahman ibn 'Awf, Abu Ubayda
> Al-Jarrah, Sa'd ibn abi Waqqas."
>
> He enumerated nine and was silent on the
> tenth.
>
> The people said: "By Allah, Abu al-'Awar,
> inform us of the tenth!"
>
> He replied, "You have urged me by Allah.
> Abu al-'Awar is in the Garden."

It is from this pattern that are derived the chivalric
Orders of Knights and the Ahl al-Futuwwah and
this in turn allows us to recognise that the essentials
of pure original nature, Fitra, have to be sustained,

honoured and protected against the entropic forces
of humanness and the passage of measured time.

IV

THE ESSEX CODE

The rich Plantagenet society, sustained, as we have noted, by familial joining and transfer, brought into being a harmonic society which through its resilience was able to survive the natural crises that threatened the continuance of its joining and transfer. King and aristocracy in dynamic conflict and collaboration were the structural grid on which the whole society depended. Allegiance, therefore, was at the heart of society. Royalty was upheld by a vibrant and active aristocracy. The aristocracy in turn was kept virile and unified by the pattern of chivalric orders and values which they imposed on themselves. Loyalty, honour, generosity, courage, and protection were the rules, goals and aspirations of the country's elite.

When the Plantagenet King John tried to upset this balance with abuses of taxation, imprisonments and de-forestation, the Barons forced the King to bow to the chivalric obligations to protect the poor and maintain the balance of society. The King was commanded to meet with them at Runnymede and forced to sign the Magna Carta.

Its two most famous clauses were upheld by subsequent administrations through from the medieval to the modern until cast down by a British Prime Minister with a degraded political class which had granted him dictatorial powers at the end of the 20th century.

The world renowned clauses, but denied today in the land of their formulation, went as follows:

> Nullus liber homo capiatur, vel imprisonetur, aut disseisiatur, aut utlagetur, aut exuletur, aut aliquo modo destruatur, nec super eum ibimus, nec super eum mittemus, nisi per legal judicium parium suorum vel per legem terre.
>
> Nulli vendemus, nulli negabimus aut differemus rectum aut justiciam.

[No free man shall be taken or imprisoned or deprived or outlawed or exiled or in any way ruined, nor will we go or send against him, except by the lawful judgment of his peers or by the law of the land.

To no-one will we sell, to no-one will we deny or delay right or justice.]

The penultimate clause of the Magna Carta revealed the chivalric honour code which had forced the King's signing and set up provision for its future observance. It decreed twenty-five Barons to be the interface between them and the King.

This clause brought out how deeply King John had betrayed both the Barons and the people. Its justice unmasked that of both King and Church. The King asked the Pope to annul the Charter. The ill-named Innocent III promptly declared it, "Shameful, base, illegal and unjust," threatening any who observed it with ex-communication, Papacy's magical last resort.

The Pope accused it of being a document which would prevent the Crusader movement. Thus Magna Carta stood for the chivalric order against the Papal system.

What the Plantagenet dynasty managed to defy

– for it was re-confirmed after King John by Edward III – the Tudor Dynasty finally brought to completion with the ultimate abolition of Papal rule under Henry VIII. The re-issues of 1216, 1217 and 1225 preserved the Magna Carta as the chivalric and civic foundation of society.

The long and magnificent rule of Henry VIII brought England into a new era. Henry's liberation of his country from the dark idol-worshipping Papal system moved events to a quite new intellectual ethos. Henry's profound reformation of Christianity was just that. If you re-form something you destroy the previous form and replace it with a new one. This was his genius. He did not see the issue as doctrinal. He opposed Luther as much as he did the Pope. His inner world was derived from his father's teaching. The Tudors went back beyond the Plantagenets to claim their legitimacy, back beyond the Normans. They derived from the ancient British King and the ancient Welsh Prince. They were from King Arthur and Prince Cadwaladr whose heraldic red dragon flew on his standard. He was the inheritor of the counter-church, chivalry. He was the Arthurian King of the Round Table, its Knights, and access to Divine Serenity on the plate from Heaven, the Grail.

Throughout his long reign he kept alive the chivalric honours and courtesies at court and in battle. Tournaments, titles, heraldry and sports all upheld the value doctrines of chivalry. At the very end of his reign he had the foolish but dangerous Earl of Surrey punished for his heraldic claim to the monarchy, as we recounted above.

True to the chivalric code and the Magna Carta he designated a Regency Council to supervise his son's place as King while a minor. Sixteen were appointed as Councillors and twelve assigned to his Household to provide aid and counsel 'when they or any of them were called.'

Although the great King Harry stands at an important stage of the structuring of the power system, astride two worlds as it were, as iconographically posed in the renowned Holbein portrait, he does not stand at the crossroads. The end of the world order that had sustained the turbulent but law-giving dynasty of the Plantagenets was fast approaching with the last days of the Tudors.

It was appropriate to Henry's chivalric political philosophy that in dying he still adhered to its Arthurian heritage, leaving a collegiate Regency. Yet so profound had been its revolutionary transformation of the State that it would take a couple of hundred years to complete the abolition of Church power. Christianity had been a macabre disease, against nature, against women and against reason. Henry in his genius saw that it was not a doctrinal or theological affair, it was about power and wealth. Far from being a tyrant as the Church-ists insisted, he proves to have been too lenient. Henry's surgery had cut the diseased tissue from the body with the Dissolution of the Monasteries. There was still to follow the long radiation therapy of Reformation until all that was left was a withered tissue of superstition on a body sedated with atheism, disguised as Anglicanism.

Against this tremendous evolutionary process, the sloughing off of christianity, the in-deep power network of chivalric brotherhood withered as a new system began to emerge. In Henry's life the dynamics of chivalric practices and style survived but with the collapse of the Regency Council almost immediately the very factionalism that only a great ruler could hold at bay burst out.

After the last Catholic convulsion of the old order under Queen Mary, the daughter of Anne Boleyn ascended the throne. So it was that in the reign of the Virgin Queen the stage was set to bring to confrontation the two fundamental doctrines of political power.

One of these lay hidden and disguised in a web of birth certificates and marriage certificates, in land ownership documents, in ritual memberships, and in military fraternities. The other was emergent, the child of successful factionalism, beheadings, and the application of natural science. In the last decade of Elizabeth's reign as Queen two utterly opposed patterns of power clashed in confrontation.

This political crisis has been obscured for two reasons, firstly because history is written by victors and survivors as has been demonstrated by the accepted record of the twentieth century's wars, and more specifically because the legend of Elizabeth the Virgin Queen became essential for all the subsequent development of the modern State. The necessity of the Elizabethan icon lay in its value as a veil over the transfer of power from monarch to a new political class.

At the heart of this transition lies the failure of Elizabeth, or rather the inability of Elizabeth to hold and protect that true zone of monarchic power, personal rule. So it was that this immense political crossroads did not show in a monarch confronting a usurping class but rather on the one hand the leading soldier of the realm, a scholar and an aristocrat, Chancellor of Cambridge University, and Earl Marshal of England, Robert Devereux, Earl of Essex and opposing him the Cecils, father and son.

The enormous presence of the scholar-soldier would be reduced to that of a foolish boy lover of a fickle but glorious aged Queen and his protagonists would continue in power, not in a zone of personal rule but caught like insects in the congealed amber of the dominant political class that would find these same Cecils struggling to rescue the political system from atrophy and dictatorship in the form of Lord Cranbourne's heroic attempt to save the Parliament's Upper House from being abolished to open the way to the end of the carefully designed political-class as governors to that of an unchecked and monarchic psychopath. In other words the Cecilian creation of a political class was to last for four hundred years. Yet with its triumph over the centuries the Regnum Cecilianum, the system designed to avoid war, became the helpless follower of a counter-system called capitalism.

The rigid structuralism of today's global crisis has both forbidden the view of narrative history, since it implies people actually are the authors of events, and pre-empted the possibility that men could change things by ideologically deconstructing the measure of man himself.

Before examining the profound and defining nature of the Essex phenomenon it is necessary to stress that the dialectic put forward by the ideologues of democracy is precisely what now demands a dépassement. The school version, if schools still persist, is that Essex represented a reactionary and backward-looking aristocratic attempt to cling to medievalism, while the Cecils represented the forward-looking middle-class attempt to keep England peaceful and getting richer and richer. What is here being examined is that the true conflict was between a State under personal rule, held in check by a counselar brotherhood of trust and honour, over and against structural rule in which nobody is to blame.

When Hollywood bought Robert Sherwood's play on the subject of Elizabeth and Essex for Bette Davis she asked for Laurence Olivier. She was given Errol Flynn. However, even at the academic level this remains the necessary viewpoint. It was very important through the Second World War which needed the Warrior Queen facing the Armada thus continuing the lie of Essex as unbalanced youth and foolish lover.

It was not until the very end of the twentieth century that this view was to be overturned, in 1999, to be precise. Professor Paul Hammer's magisterial study of Essex, 'The Polarisation of Elizabethan Politics' had as sub-title 'The Political Career of Robert Devereux, 2nd Earl of Essex, 1585-1597.' In the preface to this book its author admits that, "Influenced by the books which I had read, I thought that Essex was a kind of political butterfly – colourful and dynamic, but a lightweight compared to the sober government practised by Lord Burghley and his son and political successor, Sir Robert Cecil."

He noted that all the books seemed to confirm this view. However, when he began to delve into the manuscript evidence he "soon realised that this traditional view of Essex was profoundly wrong."

Following this ground-breaking historical re-evaluation, what Professor Hammer permits us to do is remove the Essex matter from the high drama of a personality clash to a crystallisation and impact of one ancient and natural ethos, biological and anthropological, with a new emergent model of human society that had natural philosophy as its foundation and structuralism as its identity.

V

ROBERT, EARL OF ESSEX

Robert Devereux, 2nd Earl of Essex, was born on 10 November 1565. His father, the 1st Earl, had been appointed Earl Marshal of Ireland in 1576. He died there in the service of the Queen. At his funeral it was said, "There were very few noblemen in England more expert in chronicles, histories, genealogies, pedigrees. He excelled in describing and blazing of arms." Ireland, too, was to prove the death of his son.

The Devereux coat of arms had 55 quarterings. Essex's mother re-married, becoming the Countess of Leicester, thus Essex found his step-father to be the chief favourite of the Queen. Leicester on returning to Court in 1585 introduced the young

Earl into what Wotton called 'the fatal circle'.

Essex entered the Elizabethan Court at the very centre of the value system, rites and privileges of chivalric England. It was not enough that he be distinguished by his nobility, that itself made it incumbent on him to achieve noble actions. The cult of 'virtu' united all the great qualities of generosity, heroism, bravery, justice that were the province of the high brotherhood of chivalry. His own motto was 'Invidia virtutis comes'. In 1593 a pocket dial was made for him on which was engraved: "He that to his noble linnage addeth vertu and good condisions is to be praysed: they that be perfectli wise despise worldli honor: where riches are honored good men are despised."

This, his embodiment of the chivalric ethos drove him to define his path as "The publike use for which wee are all borne." Lord Burghley, the Lord Treasurer, had been appointed as a guardian by his father, the 1st Earl.

At Cambridge in 1581 he took an MA degree.

The situation of the Court was made clear to him for his mother, born Laetitia Knollys, had re-married Robert Dudley, Earl of Leicester, and the Queen on discovering the marriage of her favourite to her own cousin sent her into a fury of rage. Immediately the Countess was declared persona non grata at Court and Leicester just escaped being sent to the Tower.

Leicester accompanied the young Essex on his first military excursion to the Low Countries. During the Dutch Campaign of 1586 Essex over that year not only had his first taste of war but was knighted. This knighthood, to one already an Earl, indicates that the chivalric initiation into a band of brother soldiers still lay at the heart of life. He returned, no longer a Royal ward, and with his step-father backing him, ready for political action.

The climax of his Dutch Campaign had been the battle of Zutphen, which not only made him one of four men made knight banneret, the highest rank of knighthood conferred on the battlefield, but linked him in legend with the great poet warrior, Sir Philip Sidney, nephew of Leicester, who was killed in the battle. Sidney's death at Zutphen marked him out to be the link and proof of chivalry, nobility and the cause of God, that is Protestant-ism. It had historically been the achievement of the chivalric ethos to abolish the Roman Church. It was at the hand of a King, who traced back to King Arthur, and with the aid of an aristocracy bonded by blood and by tournaments, jousting and Royal Tennis, that England had triumphed at last over Papal hegemony. That had been the cause to which

Sidney had dedicated his life and at Zutphen gave his life. In 1587 John Philip was to write 'The Life and Death of Sir Philip Sidney'. The book, dedicated to Essex, praised Sidney's "conquest of death by fame in his life." Sidney bequeathed his "best sword" to Essex. He also bequeathed "an other sword the best I have" to Peregrine Lord Willough-by, who was also knighted at Zutphen.

In a personal footnote the great companion of Essex saw his line continue into the 20th century, but a society given over entirely to the Cecilian quest for wealth, had no place for the Lord Willoughby of the 1960s. Tim Willoughby, loved and admired by a dazzling circle of his friends, died tragically at sea in an adventure of piracy, the only worthy activity available.

In 1590, as if to seal his commitment to the highest tradition, Essex married Sidney's widow, Frances, daughter of Walsingham. Elizabeth, of course, raged, but pretended it was because this was not a fitting bride for an Earl. His choice had not been for material benefit or prestige. It had been to seal the Chivalric Code and its new leadership.

Essex in the early years of the nineties began that series of military campaigns which soon gave him a name as a great soldier and leader. His popularity with his troops, his officers and the people increased yearly as tales of his prowess and excellence in command spread. Yet the very position he held as a general in these campaigns was due not just to his title and his Leicester connection but because Elizabeth had chosen him as Leicester's replacement.

This role of Favourite must be seen in its odd dual aspect. On the one hand it took its place as the chivalric chaste love of the knight for the unattainable matron and on the other it was the highly charged incomplete passion of an older woman for a younger man, politically not emotionally held in her power. Almost every important marriage among her courtiers was either delayed or blocked on her orders, then when nature imposed on Court ritual and the couple defiantly married they risked banishment or punishment. It destroyed the career of Raleigh and submitted Leicester and then Essex to storms of rage. Essex was twenty-four at this time and Elizabeth was sixty-two. Among the ambassadors at the Court the view was: "Mentre la Regina era chiusa nel gabinetto col Conte alle solite conferenza, chiedendozi che cosa facessero, rispondevano, 'nous tenons la chandelle à M. le Conte.'"

Privately he wrote of his longing to be relieved from "the glorious greatness of a favourite." The chivalric age was ending here, and its greatest knight was being forced to act a parody of chivalric love while still determined to fulfil the greater task of both a triumph of arms and the setting up of his own Round Table of a new nobility.

On 25ᵗʰ February 1593 Essex was sworn a member of the Privy Council. From then until his execution Essex was to experience the active opposition of the Cecils, and on the death of Burghley, the father, the scheming intrigues of the 'pygmy' son, who would in the end achieve his desired revenge.

All during this phase of his life, that is from 1593-97, the mature Essex is manifest in his activities as a protean statesman. With Anthony Bacon he set up a brilliant security network across Europe. He was held in the highest esteem and personal intimacy by King Henry IV of France and King James VI of Scotland.

In 1593 Matthew Sutcliffe in his book 'The Practice, Procedings and Lawes of Armes' wrote of the realm's chief aristocratic commander, Essex, as "the generall hope of al souldiors."

As vital to Essex as warfare stood academic activity. He loved philosophy, classical studies, and the company of scholars. The poet, Edmund Spenser, after his return from the triumph of Cadiz, wrote of Essex as "Great England's glory and the

World's wide wonder." Spenser died in extreme poverty. Essex paid for him to be buried in Westminster Abbey.

When Chapman published his renowned translation of the Iliad of Homer it carried its dedication to the Earl of Essex. Essex held the firmest conviction that political events for their fruition required not only men of action but men of Futuwwah, noble brotherhood. The letter he wrote to the young Earl of Rutland in 1595 on the occasion of his travelling abroad indicates the fullness and depths of his political philosophy. Roger Manners was the 5th Earl of Rutland and married to the daughter of Lady Essex by Sir Philip Sidney.

Essex wrote:

> "My Lord – I hold it for a principle in the course of intelligence of state, not to discourage men of mean sufficiency from writing unto me, though I had at the same time very able advertisers, for either they sent me some matter which the other had omitted, or made it clearer by delivering the circumstances; or if they added nothing, yet they confirmed it, which coming single, I

might have doubted. This rule I have heretofore prescribed to others, and now give it to myself. Your L. hath many friends who have more leisure to think, and more sufficiency to counsel than myself; yet doth my love to you dedicate these first free hours to study of you and your intended course; in which study, if I find out nothing but that which you have from others, yet I shall perhaps confirm the opinion of wiser than myself.

Your Lordship's purpose is to travel, and your study must be what use to make of your travel. The question is ordinary, and there is to it an ordinary answer, which is, that your L. shall see the beauty of many cities, and learn the language of many nations. Some of these things may serve for ornaments, and all of them for delights; but your L. must look further than these, for the greatest ornament is the inward beauty of the mind; and when you have known as great variety of delights as this world can afford, you will confess that the greatest delight is *sentire se indies fieri meliorum*; to feel that you do every day become more worthy; therefore, your L's end and scope should be that which in moral philosophy we call *cultura animi*, the tilling and manuring of your own mind. The gifts and excellencies of the mind are the same that those are of the body; beauty, health, and strength. Beauty of the mind is shewed in graceful and acceptable forms, and sweetness of behaviour; and they that have that gift do send them unto whom they deny any thing better contented away, than men of contrary disposition do them to whom they grant. Health consisteth in an unmoveable constancy and a freedom from passions, which are, indeed, the sickness of the mind. Strength of mind is that active power which maketh us perform good things and great things, as well as health and even-temper of mind keep us from those that are evil and base. All these three are to be sought for, though the greatest part of men have none of these; some have one, and lack the other two; a few have two of them, and lack the third; and almost none have all.

The first way to attain experience in forms or behaviour, is to make the mind expert, for behaviour is but a garment, and it is easy to make a comely garment for a body that is

itself well-proportioned; whereas, a deformed body can never be so helped by tailor's
art but the counterfeit will appear; and in
the form of our mind it is a true rule, that a
man may mend his faults with as little labor
as cover them. The second way is by imi-
tation, and to that end good choice is to be
made of those with whom you converse;
therefore your L. should affect their company whom you find to be worthiest, and
not partially think them worthy whom you
affect. To attain to health of the mind, we
must use the same means that we do for the
health of our bodies; that is, to make
observation what diseases we are aptest to
fall into, and to provide against them, for
physic hath not more medicines for the
diseases of the body, than reason hath
preservatives against the passions of the
mind. The Stoics were of opinion that there
was no way to attain to this even temper of
the mind but to be senseless, and so they
sold their goods to ransom themselves from
their evils; but not only Divinity, our
schoolmistress, doth teach us the effect of
grace, but even Philosophy, her handmaid,
doth condemn our want of care and indus-

try if we do not win very much upon ourselves. To prove which I will only use one
instance: there is nothing in nature more
general or more strong than the fear of
death, and to a natural man there is nothing
seems more impossible than to resolve
against death. But both martyrs for religion,
heathens for glory, some for love of their
country, others for affection to one special
person, have encountered death without
fear, and suffered it without shew of alter-
ation; and therefore, if many have conquered
passion's chiefest and strongest fortress, it is
lack of constancy in the undertaker that
getteth not an absolute victory. To set down
ways how a man shall attain to the active
power, which, in this place, I call strength of
mind, is much harder than to give rules for
the other two; for behaviour, or good forms,
may be gotten by education, and health, or
even-temper of the mind, by observation.
But if there be not in nature some procurer
to this active strength, it can never be
obtained by industry, for the virtues which
are proper unto it are liberality or mag-
nificence, and fortitude or magnanimity, and
some are by nature so covetous or cowardly,

as it is in vain to seek to enlarge or enflame their minds, as to go about to plough the rock. But where these active virtues are but budding, they must be ripened by clearness of judgment, and customs of well-doing. Clearness of judgment makes men liberal, for it teacheth to esteem the goods of fortune not for themselves, for so they are but jailors to them for their use, where we are in truth lords over them; and it makes us know that it is *beatius dare quod accipere*, the one being a badge of sovereignty, the other of subjection. Also it leadeth us to fortitude, for it teacheth us that we should not too much prize life which we cannot keep, not fear death which we cannot shun; that he that dies nobly lives for ever, and he that lives in fear dies continually; that pain and danger be great only by opinion, and that in truth nothing is fearful but fear itself; that custom makes the thing used natural as it were to the user. I shall not need to prove these two things, since we see by experience it holds true in all things, but yet those that give with judgment are not only encouraged to be liberal by the return of thankfulness from those to whom they give, but find in the very exercise of that virtue a delight to do good. And if custom be strong to confirm any one virtue more than another, it is the virtue of fortitude, for it makes us triumph over the fear which happily we have encountered, and hold more dear the reputation of honor which we have encreased.

I have hitherto set down what desire, or what wish, I have your L. to take into your mind, that is to make you an expert man, and what are the general helps which all men may use which have the said desire; I will now move your L. to consider what helps your travel may give you.

First, when you see infinite variety of behaviour and manners of men, you may chuse and imitate the best; when you see new delights which you never knew, and have passions stirred in you which before you never felt, you shall both know what disease your mind is aptest to fall into, and what the things are that breed that disease; when you come into armies, or places where you see any thing of wars, as I would wish you to see them before your L. returns, you shall both confirm your courage, and be made more fit for true fortitude, which is

given to man by nature, but must spring out
of the discourse of reason; and lastly, in your
travel you shall have great help to attain to
knowledge, which is not only the excellent-
est thing in man, but the very excellency of
man. In manners or behaviour, your L. must
not be caught with novelty, which is
pleasing to young men; nor infected with
custom, which makes us keep our own ill
graces, and participate of those we see every
day; nor given to affection, a general fault of
most of our English travellers, which is both
displeasing and ridiculous. In discovering
your passions and meeting with them, give
not way to yourself, nor dispense with yourself in little, though resolving to conquer
yourself in great; for the same stream that
may be stopped with one man's hand at the
spring head, may drown whole armies of
men when it hath run long. In your being
in the wars, think it better at the first to do
a great deal too much than any thing too
little; for a young man's, especially a
stranger's, first actions are looked upon, and
reputation once gotten is easily kept, but an
evil impression conceived at the first not
quickly removed. The last thing that I am to

speak of, but the first that you are to seek, is knowledge. To praise knowledge, or to persuade your L. to the love of it, I shall not need to use many words; I will only say, that, where that wants, man is void of all good; without it there can be no fortitude, for all other darings come of fury, and fury is a passion, and passions ever turn into their contraries; and therefore the most furious men, when the first blaze is spent, be commonly the most fearful; without it there can be no liberality, for giving is but want of audacity to deny, or discretion to prize; without it there can be no justice, for giving to a man that which is his own is but chance, or want of a corrupter or seducer; without it there can be no constancy or patience, for suffering is but dullness or senselessness; without it there can be no temperance, for we shall restrain ourselves from good as well as from evil, for that he that cannot discern cannot elect or chuse; nay, without it there can be no true religion, all other devotion being but blind zeal, which is as strong in heresy as truth. To reckon up all the parts of knowledge, and to shew the way to attain to every part, it is a work too great for me at any time, and too long to discourse of at this; therefore I will only speak of such knowledge as your L. should have desire to seek, and shall have means to compass; I forbear also to speak of Divine knowledge, which must direct your faith, both because I find my own constancy insufficiency, and because I hope your L. doth still nourish the seeds of religion which, during your education at Cambridge, were sown in you. I will only say this, as the irresolute man can never perform any action well, so he that is not resolved in soul and conscience, can never be resolved in any thing else; but that civil knowledge, which will make you do well by yourself, and do good unto others, must be sought by study, by conference, and by observation. Before I persuade you to study, I must look to answer an argument drawn from the nobility of all places in the world, which now is utterly unlearned, if it be not some very few, and an authority of an English proverb, made in respect of learning that the greatest were not commonly the wisest men. The first I answer, that this want of learning hath been in good countries ruined by civil wars, or in states corrupted through wealth or too long peace; in the one sort men's wits were employed in their necessary defence, in the other drowned in the study of the arts and luxuries. But in all flourishing states learning hath always flourished. If it seem strange that I account no state flourishing but that where there is neither civil wars nor hath had too long peace, I answer, that politic bodies are like to natural bodies, and must as well have some exercise to spend their humors, as be kept from too violent or continual, which spends their best spirits. The proverb I take to be made when the nobility of England brought up their sons as they entered their whelps, and thought them wise enough if they could chase their deer. I answer by another proverb made by a wise man, *Scientia non habet inimicom præter ignorantem.* All men that live well, do it by book or by example, and in book learning your L. shall find, in what course soever you propound unto yourself, rules prescribed by the wisest men, and examples left by the wisest men that have lived before us. Therefore knowledge is to be sought by your private study; and opportunity you shall

have to study, if you do not often remove
from place to place, but stand some time
and reside in the best. In the course of your
L.'s study and choice of your books, you
must first seek to have the grounds of
learning, which are the liberal arts, for
without them you shall neither gather other
knowledge easily, nor make use of that you
have; and then use studies of delight but
sometimes for recreation, and neither drown
yourself in them, nor omit those studies
whereof you are to have continual use.
Above all other books be conversant in the
Histories, for they will best instruct you in
matter, moral, military, and politic, by which,
and in which, you must ripen and settle your
judgment. In your study you are to seek for
two things: the first, to conceive or understand; the second, to lay up or remember;
for as the philosopher said, *discere est
tanquem recordari*; to help you to conceive,
you will do well in those things in which
you are to draw yourself to read with
somebody that may give you help, and to
that end you must either carry over with you
some good general scholar, or make some
abode in the universities abroad, where you

may hear the professions in every sort; to help you to remember, you must use writing, or meditation, or both; by writing I mean making notes and abridgments of that which you would remember. I make conference the second help to knowledge in order, though I have found it the first and greatest in profiting, and I have so placed them because he that hath not studied knows not what to doubt nor what to ask: but when the little I had learned had taught me to find out mine own emptiness, I profited more by some expert man in half a day's conference, that by myself in a month's study. To profit much by conference, you must first chuse to confer with expert men, I mean expert in that which you desire to know; next with many, for expert men will be of sundry and contrary opinions, and every one will make his own probable, so as if you hear but one, you shall know in all questions but one opinion; whereas by hearing many, you shall, by seeing the reason of one, confute the reason of another, and be able to judge of the truth. Besides, there is no man that is expert in all things, but every great scholar is expert in some one, so as your wit shall be wetted conversing with great wits, and you shall have the quintessence of every one of theirs. In conference be neither superstitious, not believing all you hear, whatsoever your opinion of the man that delivereth it; nor too desirous to contradict; for of the first grows a facility to be led into all kinds of error, since you shall ever think that he that knows all that you know and something more, hath infinite knowledge, because you cannot sound or measure it; of the second grows such a carping humor, as you shall without reason censure all men, and want reason to censure yourself. I do conclude this point of conference with this advice, that your L. shall rather go a hundred miles to speak with a wise man, than five to see a fair town.

The third way to obtain knowledge is observation, and not long life or seeing much, because, as he that rides a way often, and takes no marks, or care, or notes, to direct him if he come to the same again, or to make him know where he is if he come unto it, shall never prove a good guide; so he that lives long and sees much, but observes nothing, shall never prove a wise man. The use of observation is in noting the coherence of causes and effects, counsels and successes, and the proportion and likeness between nature and nature, force and force, action and action, state and state, time past and time present. The philosophers did think that all knowledge doth much depend on the knowledge of causes, as he said, *id demum scimus, cujus causum scimus*; and, therefore, a private man cannot prove so great a soldier as he that commands an army, nor so great a politique as he that rules a state, or a chief minister of state, because the one sees only the events and knows not the causes, the other makes the causes that govern the events. The observation of proportion or likeness between one person, or one thing, and another, makes nothing without example, nor nothing new; and, although *exempla illustrant non probant*, examples may make things plain that are not proved, but prove not themselves; yet, when circumstances agree, and proportion is kept, that which is probable in one case is probable in a thousand, and that which is reason once is reason ever.

Your L. now seeing that the end of

science, conference, and observation, is knowledge; you must know, also, that the end of knowledge is clearness and strength of judgment, and not ostentation nor ability of discourse, which I do the rather put your L. in mind of, because the most of the noblemen and gentlemen of our time have no other use of their learning but in table talk; and the reason is because they, before setting down their journey, and ere they attain to it, they rest, and travel not so far as they should; but God knows they have gotten little that have only this discoursing gift, for though, like empty casks, they sound loud when a man knocks upon their outside, yet, if you pierce into them, you shall find them full of nothing but wind. This rule holds, not only in knowledge, or in the virtue of knowledge, or in the virtue of prudence, but in all other virtues; that is, that we should both seek and love virtue for itself, and not for praise; for, as one said, *turpe est proco ancillam sollicitare est autem virtutis ancilla laus,* it is a shame for him that wooes the mistress to court the maid, for praise is the handmaid of virtue.

I will here break off, for I have both

exceeded the convenient length of a letter, and come short of such a discourse as the subject doth deserve. Your L. may, perhaps, find in this paper many things superfluous, most things imperfect and lame; I will, as well as I can, supply upon a second advertisement, if you call me to account. What confusion soever you find in my order or method, is not only my fault, whose wits are confounded with too much business, but the fault of this season, this being written in Christmas, in which confusion and disorder hath, by tradition, not only been winked at, but warranted. If there be but any one thing that your L. may make use of, I think my pains well bestowed in all; and how weak soever my counsels be, my wishes shall be as strong as any man's for your L. happiness. And so I rest, your L. very affectionate Cousin and loving friend,

R. ESSEX

Greenwich, Jan. 4"

It is clear from the famous Rutland letter that both scholar and scholarship were at the heart of his life. The renowned Henry Savile, Warden of Merton, was one of his close circle, and after a struggle because the Fellows of Eton did not want a Provost not in holy orders, he was able to get him the post. On the Queen's visit to Oxford in 1592 most of the honorary degrees conferred went to close Essex friends and allies. At Cambridge, his old college, he maintained the same lively bonds with the High Tables.

Essex the soldier and Essex the scholar do not imply a divided personality. They form the united energies of his personality. The thinking of the Latin historians interacted with the contemporary struggles he faced. Professor Hammer, who deals extensively with this dual aspect of Essex, notes: "In one instance, he claimed that Tacitus's account of Tiberius offered guidance for interpreting the likely actions of the Duke of Montpensier."

In the Preface to his friend Savile's translation of Tacitus, Savile stated: "In Galba, thou maiest learne that a good prince governed by evill ministers is as dangerous as if hee were evill himself." Essex could not fail to see that as explaining a Queen controlled by the Cecils.

Essex was a confirmed Tacitean and kept notes on Tacitus. He may also have come upon in the Annals:

"Then came a revolution in the State, and
everything was under the control of a
woman, who did not, like Messalina, insult
Rome by loose manners. It was a stringent,
and, so to say, masculine despotism; there
was sternness and generally arrogance in
public, no sort of immodesty at home,
unless it conduced to power."

The regal immodesty Essex as favourite had to
suffer was that every military exploit which took
him out of England was coupled with a bout of
hysteria from the Queen commanding his return.
These episodes increased in emotional intensity and
public displays of rage at his going and joy at his
return. At the same time Essex's military triumphs
made him the darling of the English public and the
hero of the soldiers which enflamed a reciprocal
emotion in the Queen, jealousy.

Essex saw his greatest military triumph lead
inevitably to the point of crisis in the relations
between Elizabeth and Essex.

The taking of Cadiz as well as being a military
success proved the vindication of Essex's anti-
catholic policy. Lord Howard wrote of how this
brilliant 'coup de main' by which in fourteen hours
the principal port of Spain was entered, the fleet

within it captured, and the city of Cadiz, garrisoned with 5000 men taken, was executed with the loss of less than 300 men on our side, among whom Sir John Wingfield, shot through the head in the market-place, was the only man of rank. "My Lord," wrote Lord Howard, "I assure you, there is not a braver man in the world than the Earl is, and I protest, in my poor judgment, a great soldier, for what he doth is in great order and discipline performed."

During the five years preceding the Cadiz victory affairs in England were visibly declining. There was talk of the Seymours taking up their claim to the Throne. Many spoke of Essex as the only one fit to rescue the country from its geriatric leadership, i.e. Elizabeth and Burghley. 1596 saw an uprising in Oxfordshire.

From the beginning of his military activity Essex had been gradually building up a loyal, battle-tested elite. He had conferred 28 knighthoods in Normandy, 9 knighthoods on the Azores voyage, 24 knights in Rouen, 81 knighthoods in Ireland.

What was to emerge in this final phase of his triumphs was that he set himself as representing the chivalric, indeed Arthurian principle that the ruler led from the front, that there could be no split between governance of the State and its military defence or expansion. What the Cecilians represented, for the first time, was that there existed in their post-factional ethos a governing body who sent soldiers out to fight and die for their country while a political class both stayed at home and at the same time held command of the military venture – at a safe distance. What began with the Cecilian Council, under Elizabeth's seal in London and with Essex and the noble warrior class on the battlefield in Spain, in time would be the Asquith / Lloyd George Parliament in Westminster and wholesale slaughter in Flanders. Churchill puffing his cigar in the safety of Chartwell and Wavell winning the war in North Africa. This Cecilian-mode was to reach its bloody fulfilment in Truman ordering nuclear bombs on two Japanese cities, and the notorious draft-dodging President in Washington releasing 'shock and awe' on first Iraq and then Afghanistan.

In an important document Essex set out for Anthony Bacon his position on leadership and the bond between Commander and men at war. Essex wrote:

"He that thinketh he hath, or wisheth to have, an excellent face, no sooner is told of any spot or uncomliness in his countenance, but he hies to show himself in a glass, that the glass may shew again his true likeness unto him. The same curiosity moves me to shew the true face and state of my mind to my true friend, that he, like a true glass, without injury or flattery, may tell me whether a matter or accident have set so foul a blemish in that, as my accursers pretend. I am charged, that either in affection, or opinion, or both, I prefer war before peace; and so consequently that all my actions, counsels, and endeavours do tend to keep up the state of England in continual wars, especially at this time, when some say peace may be had, and I only impugn it. But both my heart disclaims so barbarous an affection, and my judgment so absurd an opinion; and the reputation of a most faithful subject and zealous patriot, which with the hazard of my life, and decay of my estate, I have sought to purchase, must not suffer by so ugly and odious aspersion, that my actions have caused, maintained, and increased the wars, or ever had any such scope or intent.

First, for my affection: in nature it was indifferently to books and arms, and was

more inflamed with the love of knowledge
than the love of fame: witness your rarely
qualified brother, and that most learned and
truly honest Mr. Savile, yea, my contemplat-
ive retirement in Wales, and my bookishness
from my childhood; and now if time, reason,
and experience have taught me to wish that
unto myself which is best for myself, what
should I not wish rather than martial
employment, in which I have lost my dear
and only brother, the half-arch of my house;
buried many of my dearest and nearest
friends; and subjected myself to the rage of
the seas, violence of tempests, infections of
general plagues, famines, and all kind of
wants, discontentments of undisciplined
and unruly multitudes, and a receptation of
events; while I did not only leave my known
enemies elbow room to seek their own and
friends' advancement, but was fain sometimes upon trust of their protestations after
new reconcilements, to make them the
receivers, censurers, and answerers of all my
dispatches. As my affection neither in truth
is, nor, if I regard myself, in reason ought to
be set in those courses of the wars, so in
judgment I ever thought wars the diseases

and sicknesses, and peace the true natural
healthful temper of all estates. I have
thought excellent minds should come to the
wars, as chirurgeons do to their patients,
when no other remedy will serve; or as men
in particular questions are allowed to challenge combats, when there is no way but by
the sword to prove the truth of their plea,
and to obtain their detained right. Yea, I will
go one degree further, I think the prince or
state offends as much against justice and
reason, that omitteth a fair occasion of
making an honourable and safe peace, as
they which rashly and causelessly move an
unjust war.–But although wars be diseases,
yet I think better to endure some diseases,
and sickness, than to adventure upon every
medicine. I hold that an enemy may be
trusted if he offer safe conditions, as a
physician may be if he give a wholesome
and tried medicine; but to trust an enemy's
faith when his perfection shall undo, or
extremely endanger us, and infinitely advantage himself, were *medicum heredem
facere*. It is no cure to bring a state from a
doubtful war to an unsound or unsafe treaty;
it is no more than to put a feverous body out

of a hot fit into a cold. To conclude, as an unskilful physician may, by weakening a natural body by his medicines, bring it from a tertian or quartan fever into an hectic; so an unprovident statesman may, with conditions or treaty, so disarm a state of friends, reputation, and strength, as the cure may prove far worse than the disease. Therefore it is not the name of peace or war, but the circumstances or conditions of either of them, that should make us fly the one or embrace the other.

Peace is to be preferred to war; and in a state whose chief wealth, and where the revenues of the crown, arise from traffic and intercourse, where almost all traffic is interrupted by the war,—a state which in largeness of territory, and in wealth which is the sinews of war, is inferior to that of the enemy; where, besides foreign wars, there is yet a great fire of rebellion unquenched, where associates in war give over, neighbours are suspected, neutrals shew ill affection, and the people grow weary of the charges and miseries of war;—there, of all places, peace should be embraced, if it be offered and sought by honourable and fit means.

I do entirely love our soldiers; they have been my companions both at home and abroad; some of them began the wars with me, and many had me a witness of their rising from captains, lieutenants, and private men, to those charges which since, by their virtues, they have obtained. Now that I know their virtues, I would chuse them for friends if I had them not, but before I had tried them, God in his providence chose them for me. I love them for my own sake, for I find sweetness in their conversation, strong assistance in their employments with me, and happiness in their friendship. I love them for their virtue's sake, for their greatness of mind,–for little minds tho' never so full of virtue, can be but a little virtuous;–for their understanding,–for to understand little, or things not of use, is little better than to understand nothing at all.–I love them for their affections,–for soft loving men, love ease, pleasure, and profit, but those that love pains, dangers, and fame, shew that they love the public more than themselves.–I love them for my country's sake, for they are England's best ancient armor of defence, and weapons of offence;

if we have peace, they have purchased it; if we have war, they must manage it; yea, while we are doubtful and entreat, we must salve ourselves with what may be done, and our enemies will value us by what hath been done, by our chief men of action. That generally I am affected to the men of war, it should not seem strange; every man doth love those of his own profession. The grave judges favor the students of the law; the reverend bishops the laborers in the ministry; and I, since Her Majesty yearly used my service, in her late actions, must reckon myself among her men of war. Before action, Providence makes me cherish them for the service they can do; after action, experience and thankfulness makes me value them for the service they have done."

In December 1597, although appointed Earl Marshal of England in what marked the summit of his political activity and the just reward for his services to the country, there descended on him a growing factional opposition to his role in public affairs. Essex was now, in the magisterial phrase of

Paul Hammer, caught in "the enmeshing logic of escalation". His enemies had contrived not only to belittle but deny his Cadiz victory, convincing Elizabeth of their viewpoint. It was in that fierce ambience of mounting enmity that Essex attended a Privy Council meeting in the summer of 1598. The Council had the appointment of a Governor for Ireland under consideration. The Queen proposed Essex's uncle, Sir William Knollys as best suited. Essex, who wanted to keep Knollys near since he had the Queen's ear, proposed one of his enemies, Sir George Carew. The debate grew so heated that Essex rose angrily from the table, and in effect turned his back on his Sovereign. Provoked, the Queen rose and gave Essex a violent box on the ear and told him at that moment to go and be hanged! Stung at this outrage he clapped his hand on his sword. Lord Nottingham stepped up to him. Essex swore that he would not put up with so great an indignity and would not have taken such an affront at the hands of Henry VIII himself. So saying, he stormed out of the Council Chamber and left the Court.

Now this was the vital moment of truth in Robert Devereux's life. Everything after this is posthumous.

It must be understood in its finality and also in its layered complexity.

On the Queen must first be noted that she had ceded the principle of absolute monarchic authority. On February 8, 1587 Mary, Queen of Scots was beheaded. Burghley and her Privy Council had insisted and on Elizabeth's command her Secretary, Mr Davison had drawn up the warrant of execution, received her signature, sent it to the Chancellor to affix the Great Seal, and then been ordered to send it off with the Council's assurance of protection from the Queen.

On learning of Mary's degrading execution Elizabeth ran the gamut of her unbridled emotions, surprise, indignation, fury, sobbing tears. She dressed in mourning. She had poor Davison condemned in the Star Chamber to imprisonment during the royal pleasure, and had him fined 10,000 marks to his total ruin. Essex vainly tried to get him released. Of course, Elizabeth had not merely executed her sister monarch and family cousin, she had broken the undeclared principle of monarchy as God-given. This could be defined as the anthropology of kingship, the natural order of things. In Martin Hammond's translation of the Iliad it is clearly stated in Book Two:

"We cannot all be kings here, every one of the Achaians. To have each man his own master is ruin: there must be one master, one king, the man endowed by the son of devious-minded Kronos with the sceptre and the ways of law, to make judgments for his people."

Essex had turned his back on his Sovereign. This was bad manners. The Queen had struck him on the face. Unfortunately for Elizabeth, who struck about her with dreadful impunity, this was not only a sovereign striking a courtier. It was an old woman striking her young lover or pretend-lover in the publicly displayed bond of Queen and favourite. Essex drew his sword. At that moment the two contracts were broken. The 'love' contract was broken when he turned on her and it was confirmed by his mention of Henry for that meant: "I would not take this from a woman in love with me nor would I take it from a man who was King, Henry VIII, that is, the real thing."

What it meant – and here is the root of all Elizabeth's hysteria and rage and, finally, bitterness – he left her. She had not left him. There only remained revenge.

But Essex was Essex and so this end-game raised the ultimate issue – although it was one Elizabeth had sanctioned in killing Mary – that Kings, though Divinely sanctioned, were only human, and could be removed.

It was this permission which divided Kings from dictatorships. The Lord Keeper wrote to Essex begging him to go humbly to the Queen and ask forgiveness, but it was no longer a matter of court protocol. The Earl of Essex replied to the Lord Keeper at length. Here is the key passage.

"My very good Lord,– ... I am tied unto my country by two bonds; in public place, to discharge faithfully, carefully, and industriously, the trust which is committed unto me; and the other private, to sacrifice for it my life and carcase which hath been nourished in it. Of the first I am freed, being dismissed, discharged, and disabled by Her Majesty. Of the other nothing can free me but death, and therefore no occasion of my performance shall offer itself, but I will meet it halfway. The indissoluble duty which I owe to Her Majesty is only the duty of allegiance, which I never will, nor never can, fail in. The duty of attendance is no indissoluble duty. I owe to Her Majesty the duty of an Earl and Lord Marshal of England. I have been content to do Her Majesty the service of a clerk, but can never serve her as a villain or a slave. But yet, you say, I must give way unto the time. So I do; for now I see the storm come, I put myself into the harbor. Seneca saith, we must give place unto fortune; I know that fortune is both blind and strong, and therefore I go as far out of her way as I can. You say the remedy is, not to strive; I neither strive, no seek for remedy. But, say you, I must yield and submit; I can neither yield myself to be guilty, or this imputation laid upon me be just. I owe so much to the author of all truth, as I can never yield falsehood to be truth, nor truth to be falsehood. Have I given cause, ask you, and take scandal when I have done? No, I give no cause to take so much as Fimbria's complaint against me, for I did *totum telum corpore recipere*. I patiently bear all, and sensibly feel all, that I then received when this scandal was given me. Nay more, when the vilest of all indignities are done unto me, doth religion enforce me to sue? Doth God require it? Is it impiety not to do it? What, cannot princes err? Cannot subjects receive wrong? Is an earthly power or authority infinite? Pardon me, pardon me, my good Lord, I can never subscribe to these principles. Let Solomon's fool laugh when he is stricken; let those that mean to make their profit of princes shew to have no sense of prince's injuries; let them acknowledge an infinite absoluteness on earth, that do not believe in an absolute infiniteness in heaven. As for me, I have received wrong, and feel it. My cause is good, I know it; and whatsoever come, all the powers on earth can never shew more strength and constancy in oppressing, than I can shew in suffering whatsoever can or shall be imposed on me.

...

ESSEX."

In the Annals II 30, Tacitus states:

"...so rarely is it the destiny of power to be lasting, or perhaps a sense of weariness steals over princes when they have bestowed everything, or over favourites, when there is nothing left them to desire."

That same year Lord Burghley died leaving his 'pygmy' son Sir Robert Cecil to draw together all the coils that would entrap and ultimately kill his hated and envied enemy. The Earl of Essex was elected Chancellor of Cambridge, his last honour.

Hammer's study ends in 1597 and rightly says that from the fatal Irish campaign to his execution is another subject. For the significance of his life to us it is all encapsulated in the years of action. For the relevance to events themselves the tragic end has to be recognised.

The whole personality of Essex was destroyed, not a shipwreck but rather a plane crash. It is a hurtling and a plunging and a fragmentation. Yet before that tragic end he had in the clarity of his superb intellect seen the inescapable logic of power. The last issue had to be enacted. It was not ideology – that was coming soon enough – it was a deep existential insight, the fruit of a life of Futuwwah, that is, chivalric honour. It was Tacitean and by that token it was Shakespearean also. Jonathan Bate, our greatest Shakespearean scholar, devoted an important section of his master-work, 'Soul of the Age', to the link between Essex and Shakespeare. What is relevant here is not the issue of the Essex men staging 'Richard II' on the eve of their insurrection, but simply its importance lies in that a conclusion is arrived at which is that of Essex in his own age. "What, cannot princes err?" It is this insight which becomes, in his personal ethos, a decision. It is this which maintains monarchy as distinct from dictatorship. The institution is from the Divine, it is part of the 'fitra' or original nature of mankind. The holder of it is, however, answerable.

The outer issue of the split between the Queen and the Earl is a simple matter of appointing a Governor General for Ireland. The intensity, outwardly, of the issue is the factional war of the Cecilians against Essex. Given the breakdown between the protagonists, the outer issue is covered over by the historical situation, what Jane Arden called "the Other Side of the Underneath". Suddenly the sending to Ireland is not politics or rather it is revelatory of the Arden insight. Now – sending Essex to Ireland is the Queen's sentence of death. Cecil will take care of the trial and the axe. The cunning, avenging woman will send her former fixation to the same doom that destroyed his father. Essex goes to Ireland knowing it is her condemnation and his death. It follows that Essex, in returning to London and forcing entrance into the Queen's apartment while without her ritual make-up and wig, meant this to happen. Essex was not mad, but maddened. He had de-throned her, now she was a woman rejected, and seen for what she was.

The precipitation of events and the collapse of Essex himself were violent. "They found his liver stopped and perished, his entrails and guts exulcerated, and he is so feeble that to make his bed he is removed on sheets and blankets. This afternoon a general opinion is that he cannot live many days, for he begins to swell, and he scours all black matter, as if the strength of nature were quite gone."

Sir John Harrington, newly returned from the Ireland debacle, visited the Queen, his god-mother. He wrote of the visit; "She chafed much, walked fastly to and fro, looked with discomposure in her visage, and, I remember, catched at my girdle when I kneeled to her, and swore, by Jesus, 'I am no Queen! That man is above me!'"

So great were the public demonstrations that Elizabeth was forced to invoke the Star Chamber and with that Cecil was ready to do his duty and assuage his envy.

Had the insurrection succeeded there seems little doubt that he would have assumed the Throne, this descendent of Bolingbroke who overthrew Richard II, or he would have called to his inheritance James VI of Scotland to become James I of Britain. To his honour James even before reaching London on the Queen's death, sent a message releasing the Earl of Southampton, Essex's closest companion and the patron of Shakespeare, who lay incarcerated in the Tower.

Yet the affair of brotherhood among an elite was over. Cringing beside James, who loathed him, stood 'the pygmy' Cecil, as the new social order began to take shape. On the face of it, rule by committee, by bureaucracy, by structuralist system had begun.

From: 'St. Ronan's Well'

"There must be government in all society:
Bees have their Queen, and stag-herds
   have their leader;
Rome had her Consuls,
   Athens had her Archons,
And we, sir, have our Managing Committee."

                                        Sir Walter Scott

VI

THE END OF A CYCLE

"Or possibly there is in all things a kind of
cycle, and there may be moral revolutions
just as there are changes of seasons."
                                    Tacitus: Annals III. 55.

In the great cycle of chivalry, or more exactly of
Futuwwah, that is of bonded men of honour and
nobility held together by their belief in the Divine
and the obligation to service, to protecting women
and to raising up the poor, the end of its epochal
achievement is the execution of the great Earl.
Before leaving that event to look at what the next
cycle held it is important to grasp what was left
behind.

What Jonathan Bate calls the Essex men are indeed those who embody all the highest of the 'virtu' – that term which encompasses all the chivalric moral qualities. With Essex we place his loyal companion, the Earl of Southampton, the patron of Shakespeare, Chapman the translator of the Iliad, the poet Sir Philip Sidney, the classicists who gave us an English Tacitus, and the cream of a blood aristocracy that still took care of its people.

The Cecilians, headed by the deformed dwarf son of Burghley, emerged as that factional group joined together uniquely to see out the Essex men and to set up rule by committee. Without the help of one man they might not have succeeded. Francis Bacon's devastating attack and slander on Essex without a doubt sealed his fate.

Essex had counted Bacon a friend, and his brother, Anthony, had worked closely with him in his dealings with Henry IV of France and intelligence matters of the continental wars.

Essex at risk of losing his still fragile place in Council argued fiercely that Bacon be made Attorney General. He had great admiration for his intellect, and, based on it, trusted him. Bacon was certainly the motor of his execution. His enormous ambition placed himself with the new political class and at the same time upheld the doctrine of monarchic infallibility.

Bacon is rightly seen as the author of modern scientism, founded as it is on an abstract patterning and on eschewing the moral and existential, paying only a rhetoric carefully separated from the scientific proposition. One might go as far as to see in Bacon the methodology that produced the justification for the death-camp and the Gulag at the end of the Baconian cycle. What had begun as the justification to kill his friend and mentor on the executioner's block ended with the mass mathematical application of this view being used to send a race in Germany and a class in Russia to their doom. In more innocent days, Bacon had written to Essex noting: "Neither do I judge of the whole play by the first act." The first act had been friendship and the exploiting of Essex. The last act was to be treachery and the execution of Essex.

If humanism was the Erasmian attempt to have a moral code without Divine authority and a bonded brotherhood at its core, then it met its end when scientism simply swept it aside as practice leaving it only as political rhetoric.

What followed the demise of chivalry, in the manner defined here, was naturally a reactionary attempt to save it. Mistakenly, the reaction was not on the side of the Essex witness to truth, but on the Baconian view of monarchic absolutism. The Stuarts sought their survival in that doctrine as did the Bourbons from Louis XIV onwards. Significantly, Essex's son crossed over to the Commonwealth, and the cavaliers of Charles abandoned "noblesse oblige" for being beautifully immortalised by Van Dyck.

In France the last chance of honour came with La Fronde of the Grand Condé and went with his defeat which in turn led to the absolute rule of Louis XIV.

It must be remembered that aristocracy is not a signifier for moral nobility. It only is so while its members uphold the code of honour. An Earl of an ancient line can no longer be counted aristocrat once his castle houses a motor-show or a son-et-lumière spectacle. These are not the same creatures. This was the significance of Essex knighting Earls and Marquises on the battlefield. It was the knighting that bonded these men into the hidden circle of Futuwwah, the spiritual nobility of warriors. It is the splitting of governance from battle which is the antithetical principle, and the one which dooms soldiers to be sent to die by the coward-class, the

politicians, safe at home. Hitler and Churchill, both
elected politicians, conducted their war from the
safety of an underground bunker. Rommel and
Wavell had to obey, thousands of miles away on the
blood and sand of the battlefield.

The collapse of the chivalric code found its
impact muffled by the illusory, modern politics
would call it reactionary, doctrine of absolutism in
monarchy, as if by rescuing kingship one could
recover the chivalric ethos without the honourable
knights. Within that interim phase the next quite
different ethos, in which the structural State led to
a new priesthood of bankers, was slowly evolving.

The transition from the civic society of lords and
people in local areas to the 'nationalisation' of
monarchism is startlingly defined by Cardinal de
Retz.

> "M. de Rohan said that Louis XIII was not
> jealous of his authority simply because he
> did not know he had it. Marshal d'Ancrie
> and M. de Luines being ignorant were
> simply unable to inform him of it.
>
> When Cardinal Richelieu succeeded
> them he became the basis of all those bad
> intentions and all the ignorance of the last

two centuries simply to serve his own interests. He disguised them as useful and necessary principles needed to establish Royal Authority, and thus the success that upheld his plans for the disarmament of the French Protestants, victory over the Swedes, the weakness of the Empire, Spain's incapacity, let him set up in the most legitimate of monarchies, the most scandalous and the most dangerous tyranny which has perhaps ever served a State."

Once this absolutist phase had collapsed the Revolution which shook the world took over and set up its system soaked in blood. The destruction of a whole life-pattern was soon, urgently and stridently to see the construction of an utterly new one.

Religion itself was abolished as a societal factor of unification, yet it was allowed to remain as what it could not be, unless, as was intended, only the name remained. Religion, derived from the Latin 'to bind together', was banished. The nation-state took over the joining of the individuals.

Out with the Divine text, the Bible. In with the Constitution and other sacred legal texts by Committees.

Men and women, too, had to be abolished. The rational society could scarcely be founded on nature's pattern of men and women, and by anarchic extension, the family! In their place came the citizen. Individualism was born just as the 'People' became one also. The census, record of the legal citizens, rationalised access of the State to the recruitment by command of the citizens as cannon-fodder.

France as a name was tolerated despite its danger – to trigger memories of a different kind of past. The preferred name was the Hexagon. Languages, too, had to be eliminated. When Napoleon seized power French was a minority language. He himself was a Corsican-speaking outsider. When he was finally destroyed, France's frontiers were dramatically reduced from the land of Louis XIV, but on the other hand he had founded the Banque de France, as the dictator, Oliver Cromwell, had created the Bank of England. True to the expectation of his masters, Mustafa Kemal in Turkey declared: "They gave me gold and I gave them a bank."

The key part of the new structuralist system was the new elite 'Secte' of bankers. They abolished real-value money. Out went the Golden Louis and in came the paper credit-note promising to be matched against the now vanished gold. In the shortest historical span the credit-receipt paper currency was replaced by the number itself, printed on that paper. In our time that digital information has been computerised and only fleetingly exists as an electronic impulse as it flashes between two receptor terminals.

In the Old Order, ruled by the Christian Church, every child in the world was born into sin.

In the New Order, ruled by the Financial Sect, every child in the world is born into debt.

Everywhere man was free to sin.

Everywhere man was enslaved to debt.

Ownership was abolished. Corporations 'held' wealth and only allowed temporary shareholders to have temporary participation, but freed of obligation or control.

For example, Mitsubishi Corporation have fleets of factory ships which scoop out of the ocean in massive catches the blue-fin tuna. They already have a deep-freeze supply (provided the electricity is not sabotaged) which could last twenty years. In less than that this mighty fish will be extinct. This will give them a global control of marketing it at a stupendous price. The whole procedure is unreachable and so far unstoppable. Human action in the technic society is an intervention. Man is a hiatus in an automated system. Woman, as has been noted, simply had to be abolished. It must not be forgotten that there is only one woman at the high tables of banking, and she achieved this with the death of her two former banker husbands in mysterious circumstances.

It is in perfect keeping with the ideology of political democracy, where everything named actually stands for its opposite, that the woman's movement should be the mechanism for robbing women of their political power. 'Political woman' in the technic system has to be a pseudo-man, a female eunuch, transvestite, hair cropped and pitiless. The genuine power of woman, for good or evil, lies in her very persona. The truth of woman is the truth, one that cannot be submitted to systemic discipline. The Marquis de Sade was the true ideologue of the Republic. Astonishingly, or one should say shamelessly, his works are in La Pléiade edition of France's great literature. The 'political woman' who has made the cross-over to men is tolerated, but woman as woman is banished to the acting-out of the sadistic punishment or to its fantasy.

As a result of this necessary removal of woman

from the social nexus, and its replacement with the 'citizen' unit, a quite new psychology had to be invented. This was achieved by the splitting into two terms for one human condition – or rather where there had been two terms in nature, on banishing them two terms were created ideologically. Sex was separated from gender. This abolished woman and at the same time, to redesign the human landscape, introduced a third sex between the two. Wyndham Lewis specifically traced this invention to the 1930s, and recognised it as different from the natural and historical evaluation of sexual identity. He also saw that the purpose of this third sex was to dislodge woman from her place of power and set her in an open, undefined space of choices that would end, as a result, with the abolition of the family. The family, of course, being the ultimate private bank, this gave the bankers a leveraged buy-out!

With territory, a recognisable land and its inhabitants, abolished, gobbled up in catchment areas for electoral and taxation purposes –

With the family dispersed as the enemy of individualism ("You have to find out who you are!") –

With the person de-politicised from action to

alter the hegemonic banking power by granting him sexual freedom to 'discover his sexuality' –

With the social ethos of religion destroyed, all religions being equal and thus irrelevant, the personal belief system may remain since not impinging on the social nexus –

With currency virtually non-existent, a digital signal between two terminals –

With every citizen a debtor from birth to not even a debt but the deficit of a debt, itself one that through interest can never be cleared –

With all that on a planet, no longer slowly but swiftly being polluted, its air, its land, and its sea, ravaged by corporation mega-projects –

One thing emerges: the technic global system is in itself a psychosis.

In homeopathic terms it is a miasma, a zone in which the zone has become the pathology.

The proof – not all the factors above, but rather that, this being the unarguable case – not one person or group of persons seems capable of action to end the pathology.

When Libertas has degenerated into tyranny and when only those, all too understandably, who are outraged by this send their sons, the next generation, to blow themselves up in the despairing act of annihilating one's own future, and indeed leaving behind the son-murderers to continue in bitterness, when that point of nihil is reached – what is missing?

> Preference
> 'Virtu'
> Honour
> Generosity
> Allegiance

The beginning of this new cycle means the end of atheist capitalism and the opening to a new nomos on the earth.

Defenestration 1.

Defenestration 2.

VII

THE NEW NOMOS

"Still it will not be useless to study these at first sight small events out of which the movements of vast changes often take their rise."

Tacitus: Annals IV.32.

The new nomos has not vanished from the earth. It has survived. Now it is ready, yet again, to emerge into the wider arena of civil revival.

It is by the networking of groups of the noblest of youths, and the finest women, bonded together in worship of the Lord of the Universe, that the plastic and polluted cities will be cleansed. The political class will die away – it will not even be necessary to assassinate them. They are unnecessary. Their mere two hundred year rule is over. The nihil currency of numbers and scraps of endebting paper are blowing in the streets outside the deserted bank buildings. Some will be transformed into clinics and shops and even mosques, once washed clean.

Those still toxic from the miasma of capitalism will ask, "How is that possible? We do not have the strength!"

The noble youths, the Companions, newly emerged from the Cave of the 21ˢᵗ Century, will reply:

> "'How Many a small force has triumphed over a much greater one by Allah's permis sion. Allah is with the steadfast.'"

One by one and group by group they will come to support the revival of life. The binding factor, the cohering force is worship of the Lord of the Universe. The ayat of the Qur'an that has lain as if hidden up until this moment from the enslaved masses and the endebted poor will burst out in light and wisdom.

"We only sent you to the whole of mankind,
bringing good news and giving warning.
But most of mankind do not know it."

* * * * *

VIII

DEFENESTRATION

"I suspend my judgment on the question whether it is fate and unchangeable necessity or chance which governs the revolutions of human affairs. Indeed, among the wisest of the ancients and among their disciples you will find conflicting theories, many holding the conviction that heaven does not concern itself with the beginning or the end of our life, or, in short, with mankind at all; and that therefore sorrows are continually the lot of the good, happiness of the wicked; while others, on the contrary, believe that, though there is a harmony between fate and events, yet it is not dependent on wandering stars, but on primary elements, and on a combination of natural causes. Still they leave us the capacity of choosing our life, maintaining that, the choice once made, there is a fixed sequence of events."

Tacitus: Annals VI.22.

In examining the macro-cycle of Futuwwah from its inception in the medieval epoch due to the inevitable exchange between the Roman Church's religion and Islam during the Crusades, it seems that these great changes and transitions happen over centuries. Living as we do in an age of near instantaneous transmission of events a dangerous illusion has been established by the technic of media. The modern illusion is that we live in a continuum of the present. The phrase 'breaking news' is used to imbue us with this certainty that historical actions are a happening, thus they have not happened. In truth we can only hear of an event because it has happened. The news, in other words, broke.

On recognising that the warrior class could never accept a religion based on the utter victim helplessness of crucifixion and when the good news leaked

out, that it had not happened, there was a new
beginning. The bountiful, heaven-sent Table and its
Divine illumination granting Peace on eating the
Grail feast not only ended the magic rule of the
Papal regime but set up an elite community of
brotherhood and nobility.

Our modern intellect, reared on the fantasy of
swift news implying swift process in events, is
tempted to ask why these knights did not make the
cross-over to Islam immediately. Television shots
of the tsunami disaster receive the instant response
of the rescue. In the movement of the great cycles
these deep matters require both generations and
the flux of events. The key to the future freed from
idolatry required firstly the news of the Table. The
lie of christianity was in retreat from its beginning.
In its ruthless struggle to delay the light of reason
dispelling the myth of the sacraments, which in
turn determined the whole edifice of an initiated
priesthood, new doctrines were continuously being
invented. A celibate priesthood. The Inquisition.
The burning of heretics. The invention of Purgatory.
The Crusades themselves. The theological doctrines
were almost irrelevant to the issue, just as economic
doctrines merely distract from the liberating act of
closing down the bankers themselves. Luther and

Calvin had the theories. Henry VIII made the actions. The coming together of a woman he desired and his obligation to give his country an heir set in motion a change inside Henry. At a certain point it led him to see that the time had come to finish with Rome. It took him years – if the matter had been passion and procreation it could have been over swiftly. He had embarked on smashing Papal hegemony and demolishing the monasteries, freeing his country from darkness and superstition. It has taken to the 21st century for this to be established historically, since the histories were written by catholics and by writers distracted by the mercantile philosophies of the last century. G. W. Barnard's 'The King's Reformation', published in 2005, finally established that in the life of the King, Reformation had always been intended. The key action that indicated the end of Roman Christianity was the order that went out across Europe – smashing the altar of the priests, behind which they performed their bread into flesh magic. With the altar smashed – a Table was placed in the middle of the congregation.

This dismantling of the political and economic power of blood-sacrifice christianity could only happen by tremendous trans-national convulsions.

The three major upheavals that shattered the Old Order were: the English Civil War. The Thirty Years War. The French Revolution and Napoleon's Empire.

The dislodging of the Cardinals from their role as bankers soon gave way to an emergent new atheist priesthood who from their now nationalised banks began in turn to manoeuvre out the political class from power. From the unredeemable paper curren-cy to the actual cross-over from government rule to bank rule takes from the introduction of the Assignats during the Revolution to the Boer War at the end of the nineteenth century. Thus, that gigantic change in the nature of power structures took only just over one hundred years. With the Boer War, the disastrous final decline of humanism, and with it in large part the human creatures who live with an agreed life-transaction, was marked by a war whose outcome saw the political solution stalemated by the financial reality. The age of the Corporation and the Bank had begun, controlled by an un-elected personnel. Giving elected democratic governments to the masses, then fully pre-occupied with taxation, the corporation-financiers could seize the world's wealth in total immunity.

The horror of this modern age is not the

annihilation of millions in Nazi Death Camps and Stalin's Gulags, nor is it the obliteration of a whole society in Iraq and Afghanistan. It is not the slaughter and torture of the innocents. The horror of this age is the somnambulistic helplessness of the masses to ACT in order to stop the global holocaust. It is this unarguable condition of mankind which permits us to define the technic society as a psychosis. In Darwinian terms it means the species is in devolution.

Faced with the rush of events, made today to appear as torrential and the human creature as clinging on, white-water rafting under the waterfall, so extreme has it become, man can imagine that stopping to exist is an existent possibility. Suicide as action is itself madness, since it does not remove the actions, simply the actor, be it by a terrorist in a crowd or alone in a basement room.

> "For my part, the wider the scope of my reflection on the present and the past, the more I am impressed by their mockery of human plans in every transaction. Clearly the very last man marked out for empire by public opinion, expectation and general respect was he whom fortune was holding

in reserve as the emperor of the future (i.e. Claudius)."

Tacitus: Annals III.18.

Tacitus is forced to admit that if one holds uniquely to the macro-cycle of events then the meaning of existence has to be seen again as meaninglessness.

As the Raja of Mahmudabad said to this author, faced with the collapse of East Pakistan as it broke off to become Bangladesh:

"What does an ant crossing a Persian Carpet know of its pattern?"

For this understanding a new science is required which to begin with can be called the micro-cycle.

Let this science be defined as having two parts.

The first part involves the active group, or more precisely, the activating group.

The second part involves the irruption into the event of the active individual, or more precisely, the empowered individual.

Part of the message of Saladin contained this vital Ayat of the Qur'an:

"How many a small force
has triumphed over a much greater one
by Allah's permission!"

These key turning points demand three forces coming together: the time, the place and the active group.

The action of the dynamised initiators of the new may be heralding immediate good, immediate bad, or immediate anarchy. The time of this event is marked by its enunciatory character. Things can no longer go on as they were. These activators, ahead as it were of events, mark that point at which one time stops and another begins.

IX

EVENTS, DEAR BOY, EVENTS.

On being asked what might overthrow their plan, Prime Minister Harold Macmillan replied, "Events, dear boy, events!" Saladin would have explained the outer frame of events, destiny itself, as having an inevitable time-frame from the time having come until its realisation, and that time was a lunar month or any point within that month. That is between the Qadar and the Qada', the destiny and its point of event.

DEFENESTRATION

By mid-seventeenth century the Reformation had established itself but not yet allied itself to state structures in the English Henrician style. It now functioned within the vast fragmented countries of the Hapsburg ruled 'Holy Roman Empire'. It was none of these, ready to break up amid conflicting energies, religious, dynastic and most importantly, mercantile. It was a continental upheaval that began pitting catholic states against protestant principalities but ended up with a French cardinal fighting alongside the reformers against Hapsburg Austria while the financial force of the Netherlands broke free. By its end in 1648 it had claimed eight million lives. Between the emergent Bourbon and Hapsburg dynasties lay a ruined Germany. C. V. Wedgwood wrote of it: "In Germany, the war was an unmitigated catastrophe."

From Olmütz in Moravia where the Swedish Army had lived for eight years, a dazed soldier wrote of the peace, "I was born in war. I have no home, no country and no friends, war is all my wealth and now whither shall I go?"

C. V. Wedgwood related the series of actions that

resulted in the defenestration that initiated thirty
years of devastation.

"When he left for Vienna, Matthias had
given orders that any further objections
from the people of Klostergrab and Braunau were to be withstood if necessary by
force. The Catholic deputy governors immediately took advantage of these instructions
to imprison some of the more recalcitrant
burghers of Braunau. As by a magnetic force
the disunited particles of the Bohemian
opposition rushed together: Protestants
were indignant at the outrage on their
privileges, townsfolk insulted by an attack
on the rights of free burghers, and the
nobility leaped at the occasion for curtailing
the territorial power of the Church.

Thurn called a meeting of Protestant
officials and deputies from all over Bohemia
and appealed for the release of the prisoners.
When this demonstration proved useless, he
urged the Defensors of the Letter of Majesty to call a yet larger assembly of Protestants.
This second meeting was fixed for May
1618; it was now March. In the intervening

time both parties set themselves to work up the feelings of the people and of the towns-folk of Prague in particular. In spite of Catholic propaganda the Protestant meeting assembled on 21 May, a formidable gathering of noblemen, gentry and burghers from all over the province. The imperial governors in vain commanded them to dissolve. Only then did Slavata and Martinitz grasp the danger in which they stood, and on the evening of the 22nd a secretary of state escaped in disguise towards Vienna to implore immediate help.

It was too late. That very night, Thurn called on the leading nobility to form a plan of action. Overruling the protests of Schlick he demanded death for Slavata and Martinitz and the establishment of a Protestant emergency government. The city was already alive with excitement and when on the following morning, Wednesday 23rd, the Protestant deputies were seen making their way towards the royal castle of the Hradschin an immense crowd followed in their wake. Through the portals surmounted by the outspread eagle of the Hapsburg they surged into the courtyard; up the staircase the deputies led the way, through the audience hall and into the small room where the governors sat. Trapped between the council table and the wall, the crowd before and the blank stones behind, Slavata and Martinitz stood at bay. Neither doubted that his last hour had come.

Hands dragged them towards the high window, flung back the casement and hoisted them upwards. Martinitz went first. 'Jesu Maria! Help!' he screamed and crashed over the sill. Slavata fought longer, calling on the Blessed Virgin and clawing at the window frame under a rain of blows until someone knocked him senseless and the bleeding hands relaxed. Their shivering secretary clung to Schlick for protection; out of sheer intoxication the crowd hoisted him up and sent him to join his masters.

One of the rebels leant over the ledge, jeering: 'We will see if your Mary can help you!' A second later, between exasperation and amazement, 'By God, his Mary has helped,' he exclaimed, for Martinitz was already stirring. Suddenly a ladder protruded from a neighbouring window; Martinitz and the secretary made for it under a hail of misdirected missiles. Some of Slavata's servants, braving the mob, went down to his help and carried him after the others, unconscious but alive.

The extraordinary chance which had saved three lives was a holy miracle or a comic accident according to the religion of the beholder, but it had no political significance. Martinitz fled that night in disguise and Slavata continued, ill and a prisoner, in the house whither he had been carried. That evening his wife knelt before the Countess Thurn entreating some guarantee for her husband's life, a request which the lady granted with the pessimistic stipulation that the Countess Slavata should do her a like service after the next Bohemian revolution.

Murder, or no murder, the coup d'état was complete, and since Thurn had overruled many of his supporters in demanding death it was as well for the conscience of his allies that a pile of mouldering filth in the courtyard of the Hradschin had made soft falling for the governors."

Look! Look at the rock which dislodged the avalanche. In a palace. In a room. The crowd outside in a rage. Two windows open. Two politicians and their secretary are seized as passions boil over and they are flung violently from the window onto the courtyard below. The act is so specific that a word is assigned to it. Defenestration. The Shorter Oxford Dictionary defines it as: 'The action of throwing out of a window.' It dates the word at 1620, so it can be assumed that the act gave birth to the word. From it thirty years of war. From it a treaty that did at least end hostilities while it opened up all Europe's future woes. From it the enmity of Bourbons against Hapsburgs which would allow Belloc to write that the day Marie Antoinette, the Hapsburg daughter of Marie Thérèse, married the Bourbon Louis XVI, was the day of her inescapable death on the scaffold. There could be no other completion of the matter. The marriage not the Revolution determined their deaths. From the Thirty Years War on the mainland, and in harmony with the slow collapse of the Stuart regime in Britain, a new kind of creature begins to walk on the stage of events, to declare, to decree and to destroy. The Cecilian class are moving in, where men once acted for honour, courage and nobility, they now thrust forward for wealth, reputation and a fame with which only they can anoint themselves.

Antonio Gramsci, the communist philosopher, wrote in 1924 on the death of Lenin, "Every State is the dictatorship of a small number of men, who, in their turn, organise around one from among them." Luciano Canfora insists that this Gramscian definition applies equally to contemporary democracies. The political class are uniquely the servants of a financial oligarchy. Their task is to encase the oligarchic tyranny in the illusion of a choice which licenses the on-going dominance of high capital.

There are, therefore, today, two power groups in total, yet rarely apparent, control of world affairs: the bankers and the mafiosi. Beneath them, their servants the political class face the masses, taking the bullets and a modest wealth, while their effective leaders get initiated into worthless but remunerative Foundations of supra-national status.

Our present situation dates from the collapse of the Futuwwah among a knightly elite at the end of the Elizabethan Age and the havoc of European wars. The guillotining of Marie Antoinette forced Edmund Burke to his famous protest: "The age of chivalry is gone: that of sophists, economists and calculators has succeeded, and the glory of Europe is extinguished for ever." Of course, the demise of chivalry must be set back to its true end with the failure of the Essex coup d'état, yet the French Revolution allowed its tragic demise to re-echo in the popular consciousness.

Alongside the relevance of Gramsci one must set another communist ideologue, Trotski, who declared what is now axiomatic in modern politics, that in the future there would be no personal rule only committee empowerment. Structurally, in the democracies, this became the case. Existentially, Gramsci's insight goes deeper, since all finally devolves on one man, as Homer had warned the Greeks in the Bronze Age.

What we now participate in is the tragedy for mankind that that leadership is valueless, without honour and virtu, so that the active guide of such an elite can only drive the masses to destruction.

Look now at that second defenestration which took place at the Führerbau in Munich, 1938. The window itself and the dung heap below were now mere metaphors, but certainly appropriate. It could not have happened if it had not been preceded by a watershed in the history of Germany just before the fated reunion.

Field Marshal Werner Freiherr von Blomberg,

Hitler's Minister of War and Commander-in-Chief of the German armed forces, and Colonel General Freiherr Werner von Fritsch, Commander-in-Chief of the army, were both mired in separate sexual scandals. Hitler announced that both had resigned on health grounds. "From now on I personally will take over the command of the whole armed forces." The War Ministry was abolished. Hitler appointed himself Supreme Commander of the Wehrmacht. The political class had stepped up to the dais of military command. It was to be this apotheosis which characterised the whole political model of the twentieth century. Hitler in Germany. Churchill in Britain. Roosevelt in the USA. Stalin in Russia. And finally Mao in China. Hitler forced Rommel to suicide. Churchill disgraced Wavell. Stalin smashed his military High Command. Truman fired MacArthur and Mao swept away Chiang Kai Sheck. The rats had risen from the fetid hold of the Assembly and taken over the bridge of the ship of state. So it was to continue into the 21st century with Blair degrading the British High Command and Obama sacking McChrystal, his only viable General. It was now the modus operandi of 'democratic' governance.

The Munich conference took place at the

Führerbau. Closeted in that room were only a handful of men. On neither side were its decisions dependent on an outside veto or critique. The drama of Munich is that it was a defenestration, once done there was no democratic or personal intervention. It was a fait accompli.

Present were, in huis clos:
Adolf Hitler: Reich Chancellor
Edouard Daladier: President of the
    French Council
Sir Neville Chamberlain: British Prime Minister
Benito Mussolini: President of the
    Italian Council
Alexis Léger: Secretary General of the
    Quai d'Orsay
Sir Horace Wilson: Personal Adviser
    to Chamberlain
Count Galeazzo Ciano: Italian Foreign Minister
Joachim von Ribbentrop: German
    Foreign Minister
Paul Schmidt: interpreter
Field Marshal Hermann Göring;
    2nd in Command of the Reich
Sir Neville Henderson; British Ambassador,
    Germany

Frank Ashton-Gwatkin: British Diplomat
André François-Poncet: French Ambassador,
  Germany
Charles Rochat: Diplomat, colleague of Léger
Marcel Clapier: Daladier's Cabinet Chief
Captain Paul Stehlin: Air Attaché,
  Berlin Embassy

The Germans totally overwhelmed the Franco-British team. Hitler said: "Chamberlain! That senile old rascal. If ever that silly old man comes interfering here again with his umbrella, I'll kick him downstairs and jump on his stomach in front of the photographers." Defenestration.

Millions of dead soldiers and civilians later, with the near genocide of a race by the Germans and of a class by the Russians, Europe lay in ruins. The British Empire was destroyed utterly by the USA, and in Europe Germany won, transformed into its new financial power house.

Rudyard Kipling, who lost his son in World War One, had written:

"If any question why we died
Tell them, because our fathers lied."

In place of honour had come dishonour. In place of truth had come lies. In place of service had come seizure. In place of an arena of shared brotherhood had come an arena of profit acquired.

Never more than today do the oligarchic elite and their public relations machine, elected democracy, lay claim to moral values and endlessly preach these values. Civilisation is a pet word of the media-driven discourse. It is, alas, beside the point.

"Magis alii homines quam alii mores."
Tacitus; Hist. 2.95
"Rather different men than different values."

The creature has devolved, diminished, and may soon disappear. This restoration of an evolutionary curve against the entropic plunge of the human into the sub-human – is still possible. Against such a possibility stand the vast billions of mass man, atheist, slave to chance, gambler, the rat worshipping hindu, the cat and dog devouring, bear torturing Chinese, the psychopathic American. All that is required is one enlightened man to connect in that harmonic movement of crystallisation which draws together a few like men, as the iron-filings move together and organically merge in a complex geometric patterning. Each in turn will have had a memory of great love. There will always be an initiator.

At this point only a personal anecdote will be acceptable as evidence.

"I was waiting in the café of a Madrid hotel, breakfasting ahead of a meeting. I was approached by a young Mexican who crossed over to my table and asked permission to join me. He was courteous and I motioned him to sit. He told me he was on a pilgrimage to Europe to visit its greatest living writer. When I asked he told me it was Ernst Jünger. I explained that he was a friend of mine. Soon in discussion of Jüngerian themes he told me of his experience in Mexico. Following the tre-mendous earthquake which devastated Mexico City the public soon realised that the State and the political apparatus were helpless and unable to come to the rescue. Then something happened. Something quite new. A doctor stepped forward among the ruins. He called for nurses. In a moment two other doctors offered their help. A contractor said he could organise the removal of rubble to reach those trapped. Another person began to set up a food service unit. In the shortest time the people were working together, from every kind of capacity, help was coming forward. They were the rescue. They were the local community. They had become the State, and the structuralist State had simply disappeared."

It is this mutual recognition and coming together in a crystallisation of unplanned and unpredicted harmonics that is the basis of what Ibn Khaldun called Asabiyya, the joining of the elite brother-hood, the raising up of the human situation into something higher, something luminous.

At the end of Shakespeare's tragedy, 'Hamlet', as the action finally arrives at its completion in the last great scene Hamlet is able, after all his tormented experience, to complete what he has struggled throughout the play to accomplish. Hamlet is killed, of course, but so too are the King, the Queen and Laertes. Horatio is left to tell the world how it was, despite everything, a matter achieved and completed. The Kingdom is purified, and Fortin-bras enters heralding purification and renewal.

Before the last great resolution of the drama, Horatio questions Hamlet as to what stage the affair has reached.

> Horatio: It must be shortly known
>   to him from England
>   What is the issue
>   of the business there.
> Hamlet: It will be short:
>   the interim is mine;
>   And a man's life's no more
>   than to say "One."

* * * * *

It is told of the Baron de Sigognac whose vineyards produced the Armagnac brandy that one day he took all the clocks out of his cellar. He had a set of new clocks made. On these clocks the face had ten divisions instead of twelve. The seconds had become years and the big hand moved only once a decade while the hour hand marked the centuries. With time, however, the Baron came to trust only his own palate in telling the age of the Armagnac. The clocks were abandoned, left unwound. The Baron de Sigognac himself had become the memory of his Armagnacs and their embodiment.

* * * * *

Repeat after me: it is all, all contained in me. Now I must act. It will be short, but the interim is mine.

* * * * *

SELECTED BIBLIOGRAPHY

The Polarisation of Elizabethan Politics: Paul Hammer
(Cambridge)
Wavell: Supreme Commander: John Connell (Collins)
Wavell: Scholar and Soldier: John Connell (Collins)
The Thirty Years War: C. V. Wedgwood (Folio)
Folio Complete Works: ed. Bate & Rasmussen
(Modern Library)
Soul of the Age: Jonathan Bate (Random House)
The King's Reformation: G. W. Bernard (Yale)
Plantagenet England: Prestwich (Oxford)
Chivalry: M. Keen (Yale)
Henry VIII's Last Victim: J. Childs (Cape)
The Roman Revolution: Ronald Syme (Oxford)
Annals and Histories: Tacitus (Everyman)

* * * * *

PLATES

Robert Devereux, 2nd Earl of Essex after Marcus Gheeraerts
the Younger (1596): National Portrait Gallery

The Defenstration of Prague in 1618: engraving
Matthaeus Merian the Elder, from 'Theatrum Europaeum',
Frankfurt, 1662 (Universitätsbibliothek Augsburg)

Munich, 1938: David Faber, Simon & Schuster

* * * * *

The quotations from the Quran are taken from:
The Noble Qur'an – a new Rendering of its Meanings in
English, translated by Abdalhaqq and Aisha Bewley